His Most Exquisite Elaborations

I0471814

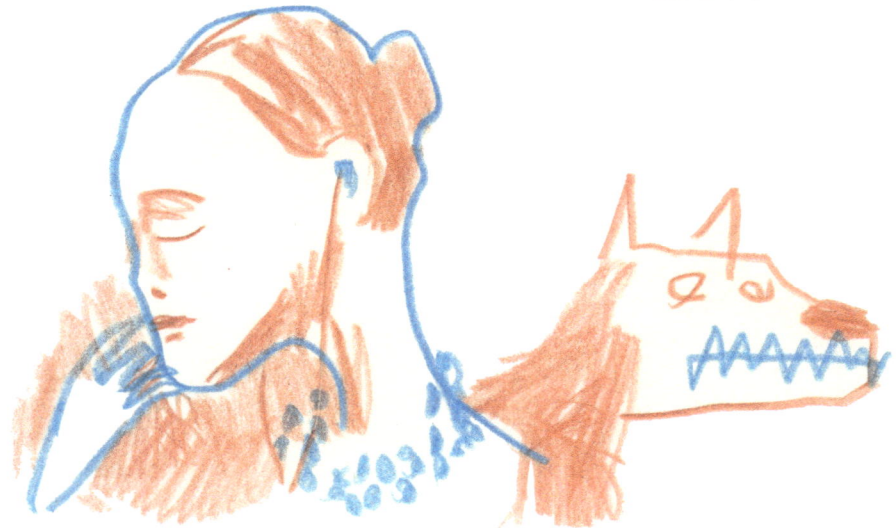

Artwork by Johannes Mundinger-XXcrew

Published by Idrawalot
PO Box 16744 Seattle WA 98116-0744

ISBN: 978-1468190441

All rights reserved.
Without limiting the rights under copyright reserved above, no part of this publication may be reproduced, stored in or introduced into a retrieval system, or transmitted, in any form or by any means (electronic, mechanical, photocopying, recording or otherwise), without the prior written permission of the copyright owner.

Idrawalot books are available through direct distribution and are also available in a variety of electronic formats. To contact Idrawalot directly write to addison@idrawalot.com

Title: His Most Exquisite Elaborations
Author: Johannes Mundinger, xXcrew
Publisher: Idrawalot
Address: PO Box 16744 Seattle WA 98116-0744
Format: Paperback
Publication Date: January 2012
ISBN: 978-1468190441

www.jmundinger.de
idrawalot.com

Ich schaue Kunst auch für Sie

I'll look at art for you as well
(Johannes Mundinger)

The rain always hammered in the same rhythm against the window. It was one of those long, weary mornings at the office. A day where the phone refused to ring, a day that would have been best begun with a decent sip - straight from the bottle in my desk - of a single malt. The sign on my door declared "Office for Art Mediation." It may as well have said nothing at all. Simply another anonymous door, like thousands of others in this and any cities in the world. Well, if there's to be no whisky, then at least a bit of coffee, doubtless the 135th. On top of that, the bank was at my heels and I considered how I could get my hands on a few dimes, to pay the coffee machines next refill. The doorbell pulled me out of my thoughts. I got up from the desk and pressed the buzzer. A short time later the door opened and a head of tousled brown curls, piercings included, pushed itself through the door, followed by a Libertine's shirt, a pair of jeans, and the unavoidable pair of Chucks.

"Office for Art Mediation? Am I in the right place?"
"Well, it says so on the door. What can I do for you?"
"I came across an exhibition and encountered an artist. And now I'd really like some information about him and his work, would you be able to help me? And how much would it cost?"
"Of course I can take the case. That's what I'm here for. It will, however, cost 150 Euros per day plus expenses."
"That's no problem."

She put five hundred on the desk. At least the coffee was guaranteed now.

"Will that be enough?"
"Certainly. Which artist are we talking about?"
"He's called Johannes Mundinger and the only thing I know is that he lives in Berlin."
"Ok, that's enough for a start. Leave your number here, and I'll contact you as soon as I have something."
"Thanks!"

She wrote her number on a Post-it, got up and exited with a none too exaggerated wiggling of the derrière.

I lit up a cigarette and asked myself, whether something like God might exist after all. I had an assignment. And I was back in the black. For the time being. Ok, how to start? Naturally with the unavoidable foundation of every investigation: Google. So I signed out of Youporrn and opened the data oracle and entered "Johannes Mundinger." The first thing that came out was jmundinger.de. Current Work Projects and Exhibitions by Johannes Mundinger, all lucidly arranged in a blog: Illustrations and To Be Exhibited, it was called.

I clicked through the site. Full of activity and incredibly vivacious. But firstly I'd have to have a few facts about this guy My suspicion about active artists seemed to be confirmed: even in 1982 - his year of birth - he was already up and at it with his first drawings. I tried not to think about what kind of drawings they were. An unpleasant association with spinach popped up in my mind anyway. There was also something about the Black Forest, Offenburg, studies in Lahr, Muenster and Brussels. The kid knew what he was doing and could spare himself the usual pleads of ignorance. This hunch was strongly confirmed with a long list of exhibitions, but I couldn't shake that recurring feeling of doubt, that he was making fun of the whole holy CV obsession in the arts business. Under the list of prices could be read: 1992, Lego Knight with Horse from a Christmas Raffle, Herti, Offenburg. Not entirely what one expects from the context.

I knew enough now to take a closer look at what he does. Relatively quickly it became clear to me that he had started with graffiti and clearly not classical nude sketches. Hot on the tail of this information, I began to have a look at a few of the pictures. To me, they didn't seem entirely to be typical of the genre, but reminded me of Jean Michel Basquiat in their treatment of surface, form and line. Instead of the usual mish-mash of name tagging with clear cut outlines, the lines here became independent from their form, growing wildly all over the place. The multi-layered picture scape was given geometric patterns, fragments of text and sentences, often combined with contradictions like illustrative elements full of childish charm with hard, crudely applied color patches and octopus drawings. A three eyed monster that looked like the illegitimate child of the Cookie Monster and Robert Crumb regularly cropped up. More often than not it picked the nose of other figures that mostly had a sketched, unfinished quality. The relics of the painting process, such as streaks and sprays, matched the drawn figurative elements that were simply put on the drawing surface. Through it, a multidimensional pictorial space emerged, one that did not attempt to evoke the illusion of depth and space. Here was someone at work who no longer had to prove that he could draw and knew what he was doing. He casually helped himself from the trove of drawings in art history and pop culture. Well, my first impressions were not erroneous. Then there it was, the untoppable proof of my hunch, that Basquiat was serving as the point of reference for this jungle of drawings and colors. In an act of appropriation he used typical elements of the New York artist. Even his name was there to be seen. But it was not the a lesser imitation, but the single, seemingly discordant elements like The Cookie Monster's Son, and the Red Turnip Nose, which were combined to create a tasty visual scrambled egg. It led to a heterogenous, polyphonic picture as a whole. His joy in maskings, (re-)mixing and playfulness was what reminded me of Bachtin's concept of the Carnival.

Ok, what else does this schmuck have to offer? In the hope of new information I scrolled down the page and stopped at a series of Stickers. There were the bubblegum dispensers, that - in the days of telephone cards and condom vending machines - seemed like relics of a long lost time, and were to me like those cookies in that boring novel, pretending a trip back in time to one's own childhood. Damn, had this guy discovered a hidden door, behind which the space-time continuum no longer existed? Simply because he cut out a bit of paper and decorated it colorfully? It's getting more and more absurd.

Then there were the signs that added to my suspicions. Signs normally assist in orientation, but these here led instead to a short circuit in my head. They simply depicted the reality and actually led to their own existence. They were the self-referential, painted imitations of signs, with real stickers plastered on. Reality and depiction simultaneously. It was too much for me. A dull hammering began in my skull. I massaged my temples, got up to make a coffee, lit up a cigarette and gave myself a break. Man, this guy wasn't to be underestimated.

After a while I had calmed down enough to continue. I decided to look at the Chatroulette Portraits next. It was different to the works I had previously seen, and didn't undertake artistic work in public space. On the contrary, it took the openness of the internet into the private artistic process. Similar to the wall pictures the individual pictorial elements corresponded with one another, but they were in the furthest autonomously related. Their hastily thrown together lines of portraits in fleetingly colored surfaces corresponded to the quick lived medium, from which their subjects were taken. Digital space made to be experienced through analogue means.

As I looked around, I came upon a few works that left their surface completely and expanded in space, like the papier-mâché aesthetic of the installation reminiscent of The Science of Sleep. This aesthetic was consequentially maintained in other installations, for instance, the sprayed cartons in Need for Speed 2.0, that put a track toy care in an urban environment or a hut made of roof tiles and cartons in a parking lot and tested the intellect of the office of public order sorely.

Slowly I got the impression that every medium was appropriate and the most profane materials were just the right thing. They were best paired with banal themes, like in the example of Nose Picking Pictures. Was it about the avoidance of collaboration with a sublime artistic concept with a bloated theoretical superstructure? Was it simply the joy in creating in the moment without having to consider the reception in the world afterwards? Is the artist picking my nose with his index finger, in order to consume the last traces of the grey matter in my head for dessert with delight?

I took a sip of coffee, took the slip of paper and called the number.
"Yes?"
"Breitenstein. Office for Art Mediation. It's about Johannes Mundinger. I just wanted to give you a short report. But I really have to warn you..."

Oliver Breitenstein
Director Berliner Kunstverein

Translation: Flora Suen

http://en.wikipedia.org/wiki/The_Libertines
http://en.wikipedia.org/wiki/Jean-Michel_Basquiat
http://de.wikipedia.org/wiki/Robert_Crumb
http://en.wikipedia.org/wiki/Mikhail_Bakhtin
http://en.wikipedia.org/wiki/The_Science_of_Sleep

Ibug
<u>Industriebrachenumgestaltung</u>
<u>PALLAS WERKE, Meerane, 2011</u>

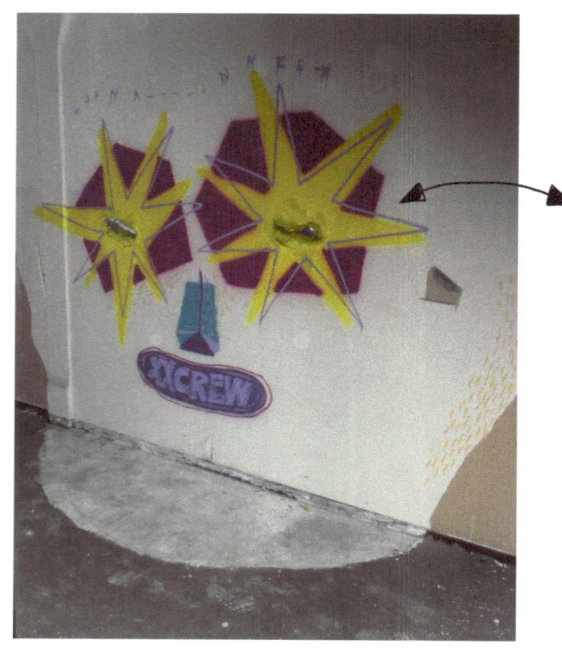

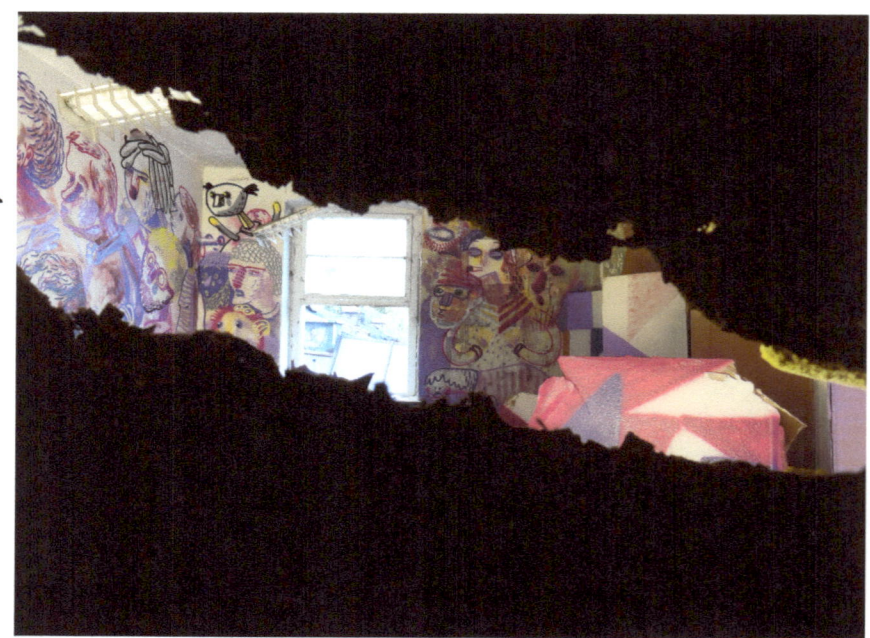

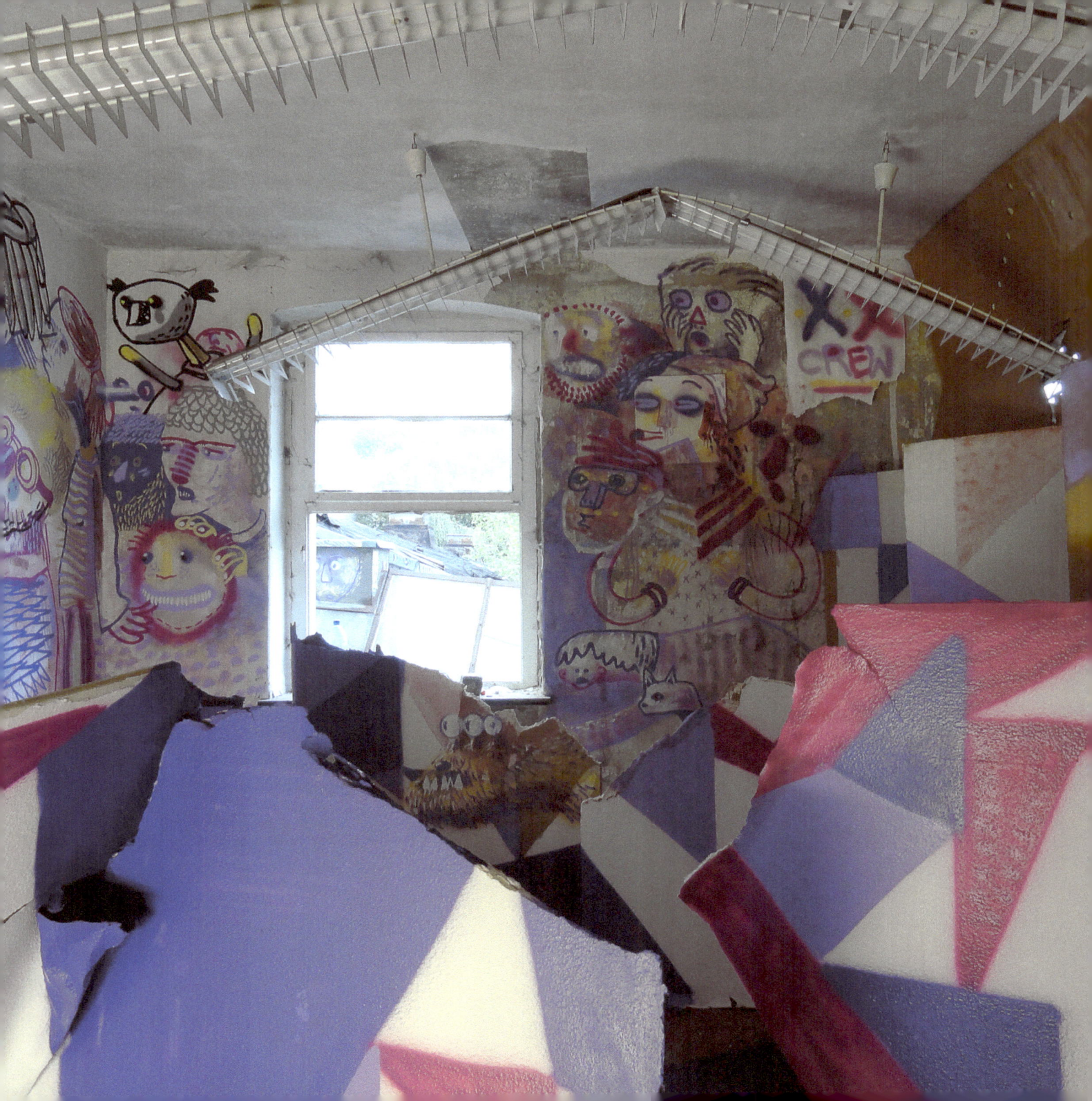

PRODUKTION AUSWURF
with Peter Bröcker & Wilm Lindenblatt
GALERIE KREUZBERG, Münster. 2010

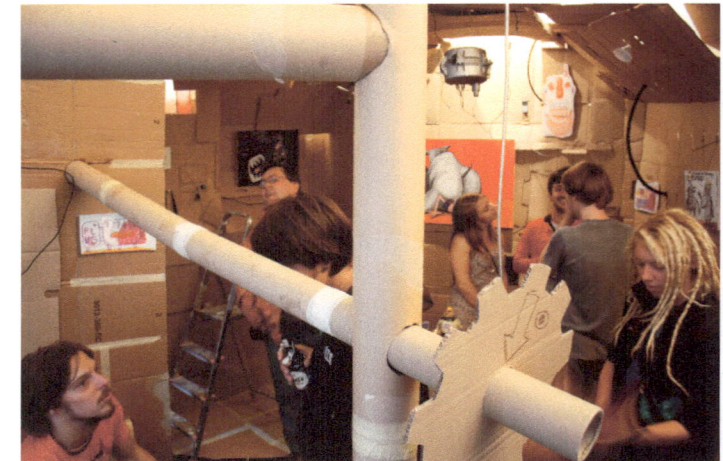

"The only permanent kind of earthly felicity is the consciousness of productivity," said Carl Zuckmayer.

Are machines lucky? May a humanoid machine acquire felicity? "Will happiness find me?" (Fischli/Weiß) even if i'm a machine?

VERFOLGUNGSJAGD 2.0
with Berliner Kunstverein and Dirk Sandbaumhütter
CUBA KULTUR, Münster, 2010

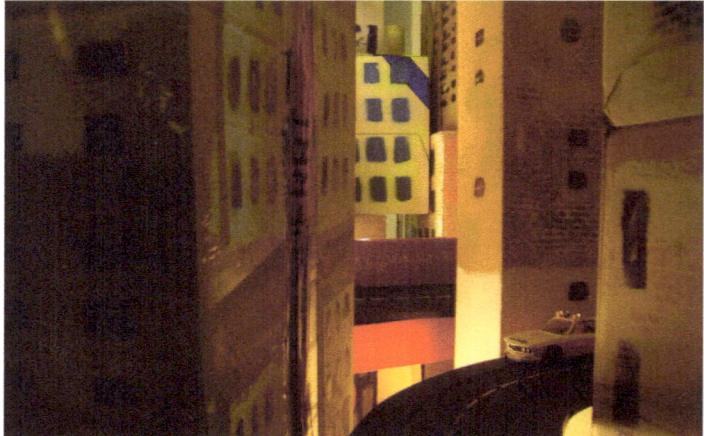

Several artists were working on the topic of an <u>auto pursuit</u> for a five-day long exhibition. Everything revolved around the following: carrera-races, playing testdrive (c64) or reading comics about auto-pursuits. Streetartist, musicians and authors "pimped" the cutural center.

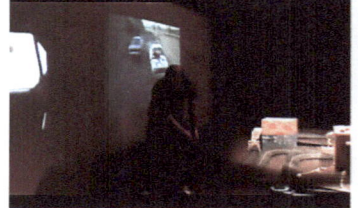 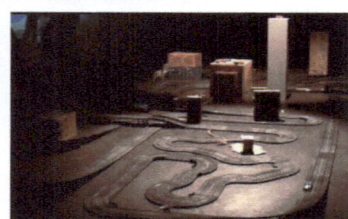

WHOLECAR
xXcrew Soloshow
GALERIE KESSELHAUS, Lahr, 2010

For their "xXcrew - Solo Show" the xXcrew built their own wholecar. A 26-meter long homage to their past, an (almost) exact copy of the German N-Waggon Minze, was made ready to be colored.

→

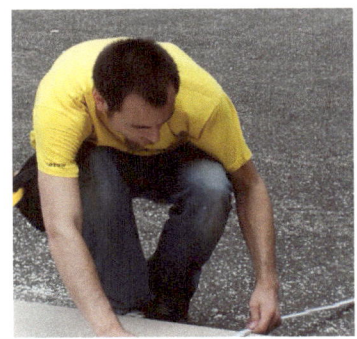 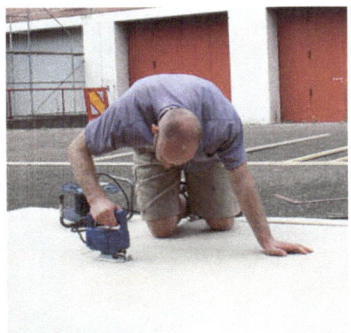 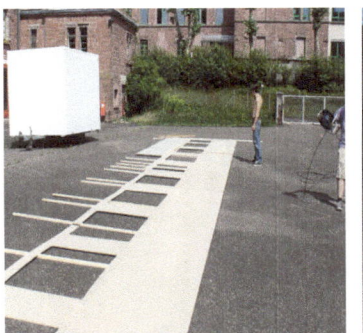 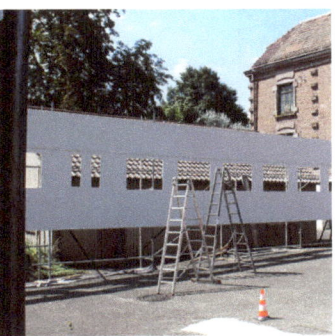

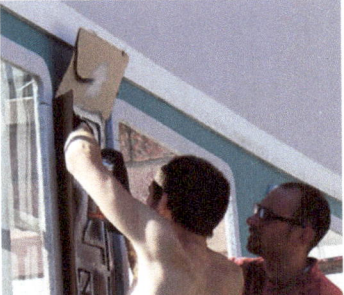 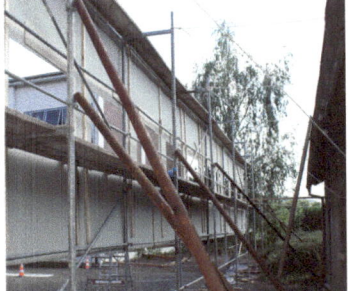 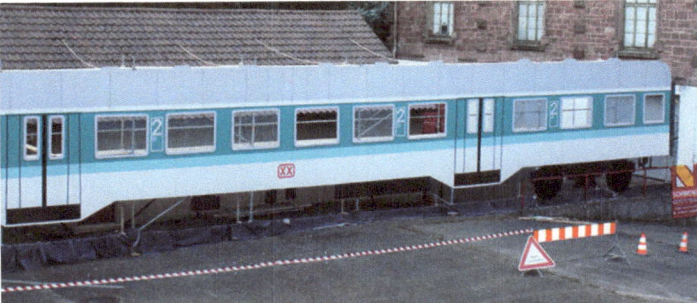

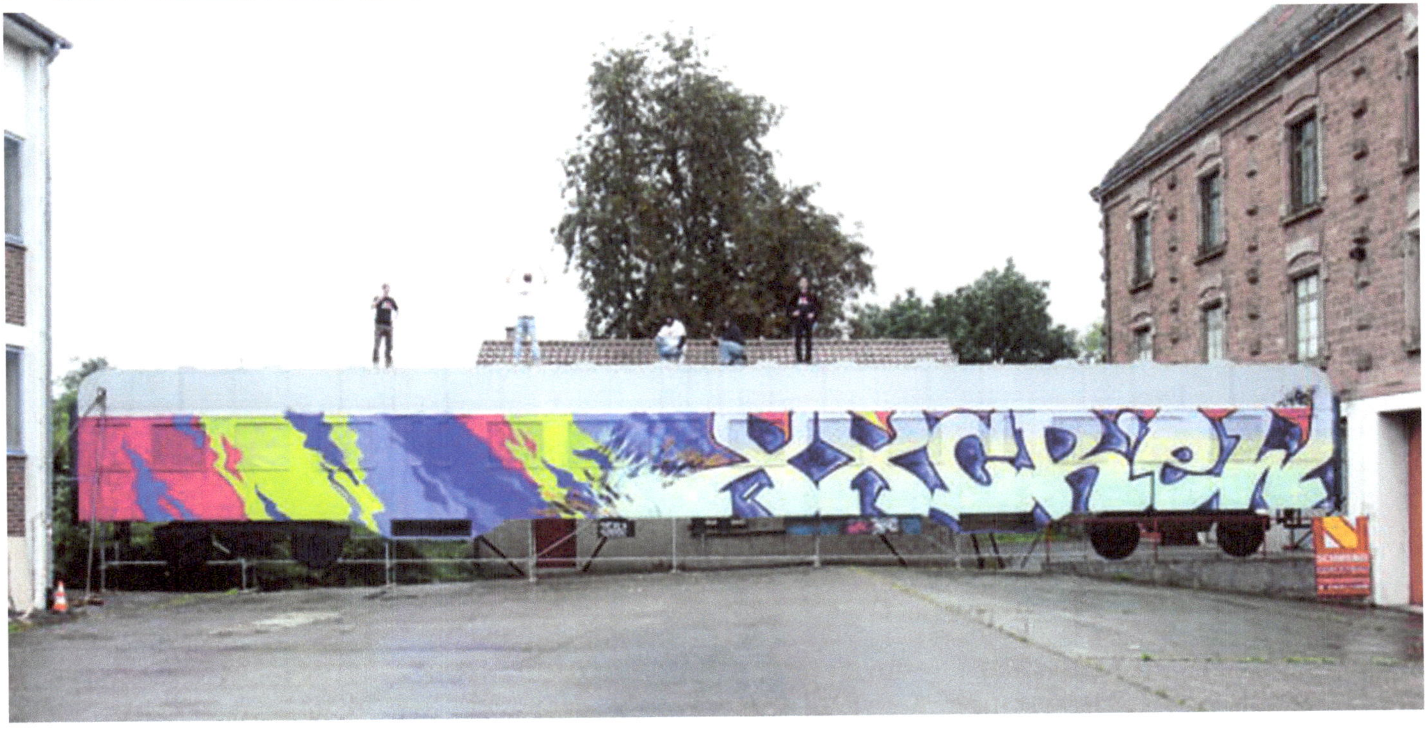

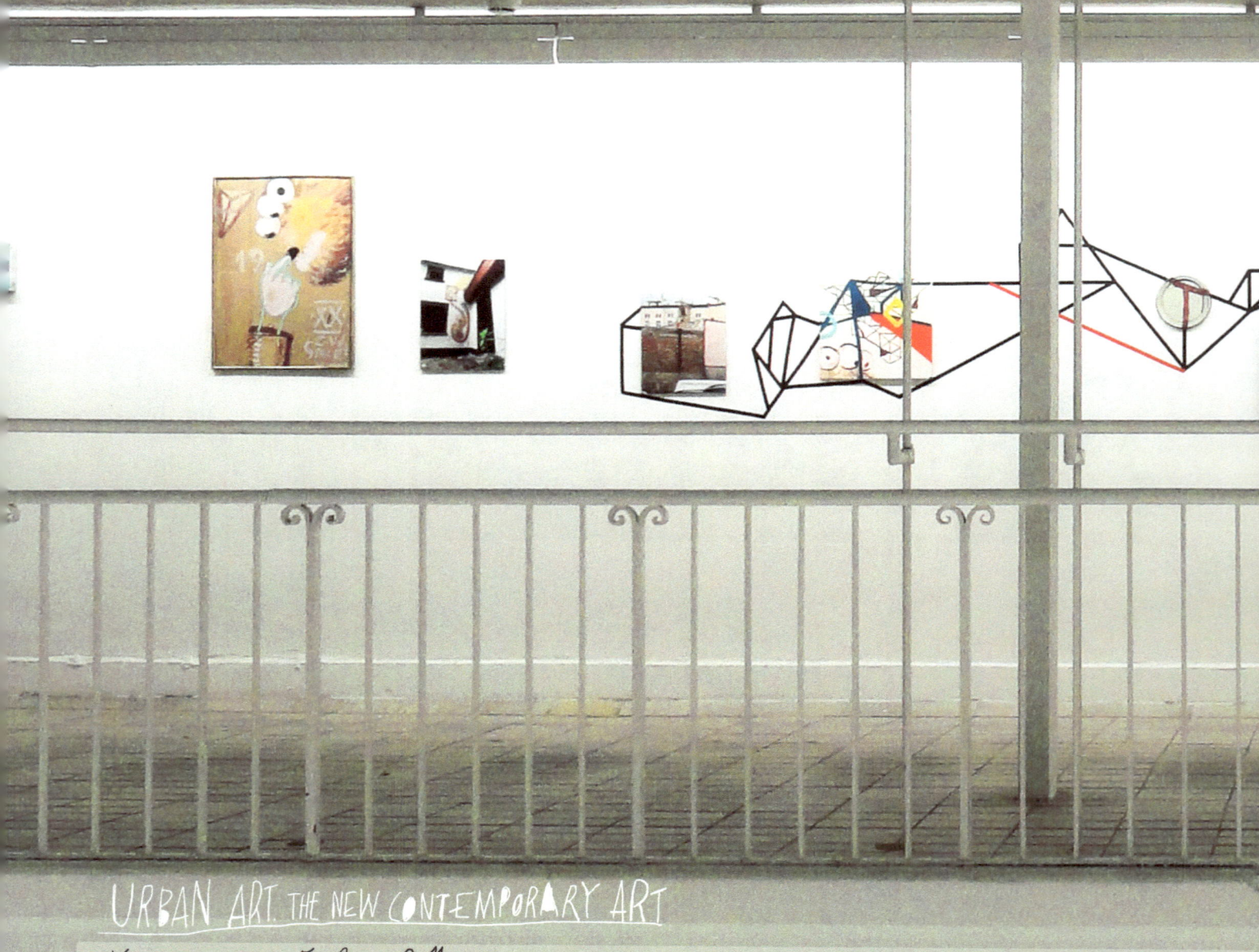

URBAN ART. THE NEW CONTEMPORARY ART

KUNSTVEREIN Freiburg 2011

The members of the Kunstverein were pleased with this new approach (urban art) and the exhibition. The only exception the curator remembers: don't such works of art lose something, if you put it into a gallery? That's the topic Johannes Mundinger was working on; he interpreted "Urban Art Goes Gallery" literally. The surfaces he painted on - lids, old frames, wood - were found on the streets, integrated them in his murals and took them back to the gallery. His works show these parts, photos of the whole murals and - streetart-style - the wall of the gallery

Sarah Nagel, BZ 19.09.2011

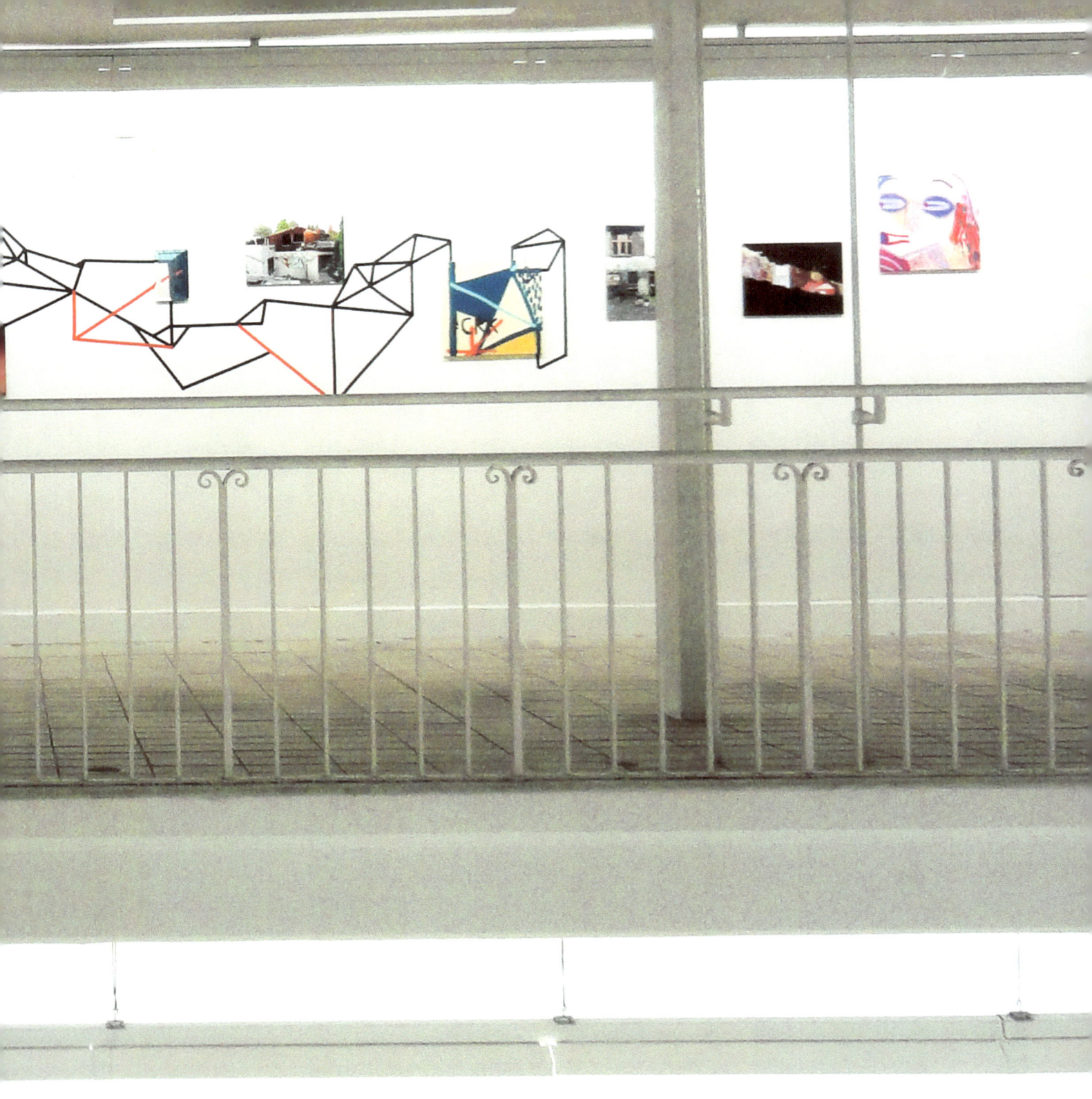

o.T. (Asozialer Wohnungsklau)
with Pio Rahner

POLLY POCKET MUSEUM of MODERN ART

Berlin 2010...

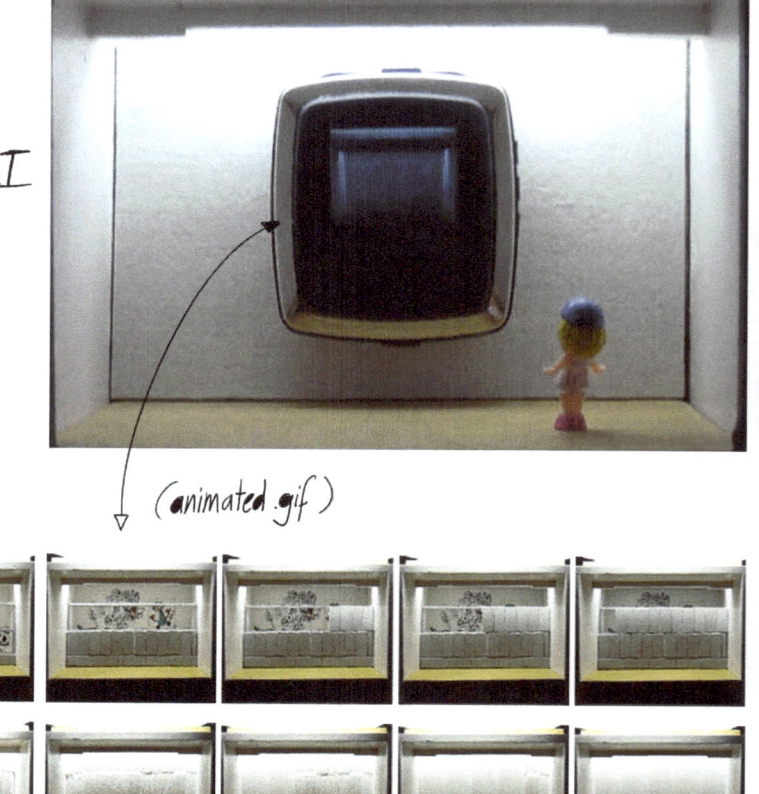

(animated .gif)

ENCORE ET TOUJOURS

CENTRE CULTUREL, DINANT, B 2011

After Bruxelles (2009) and Münster (2010), six young artists coming from different European countries have chosen the Regional Cultural Centre of Dinant for working together on a group exhibition. The themes? The flying time, repetition, erosion, delay...

The group consists of Elias Errerd, Raphaëlle Goffaux, Florian Kiniques, Johannes Mundinger, Agata Stepien and Sébastien Wouters.

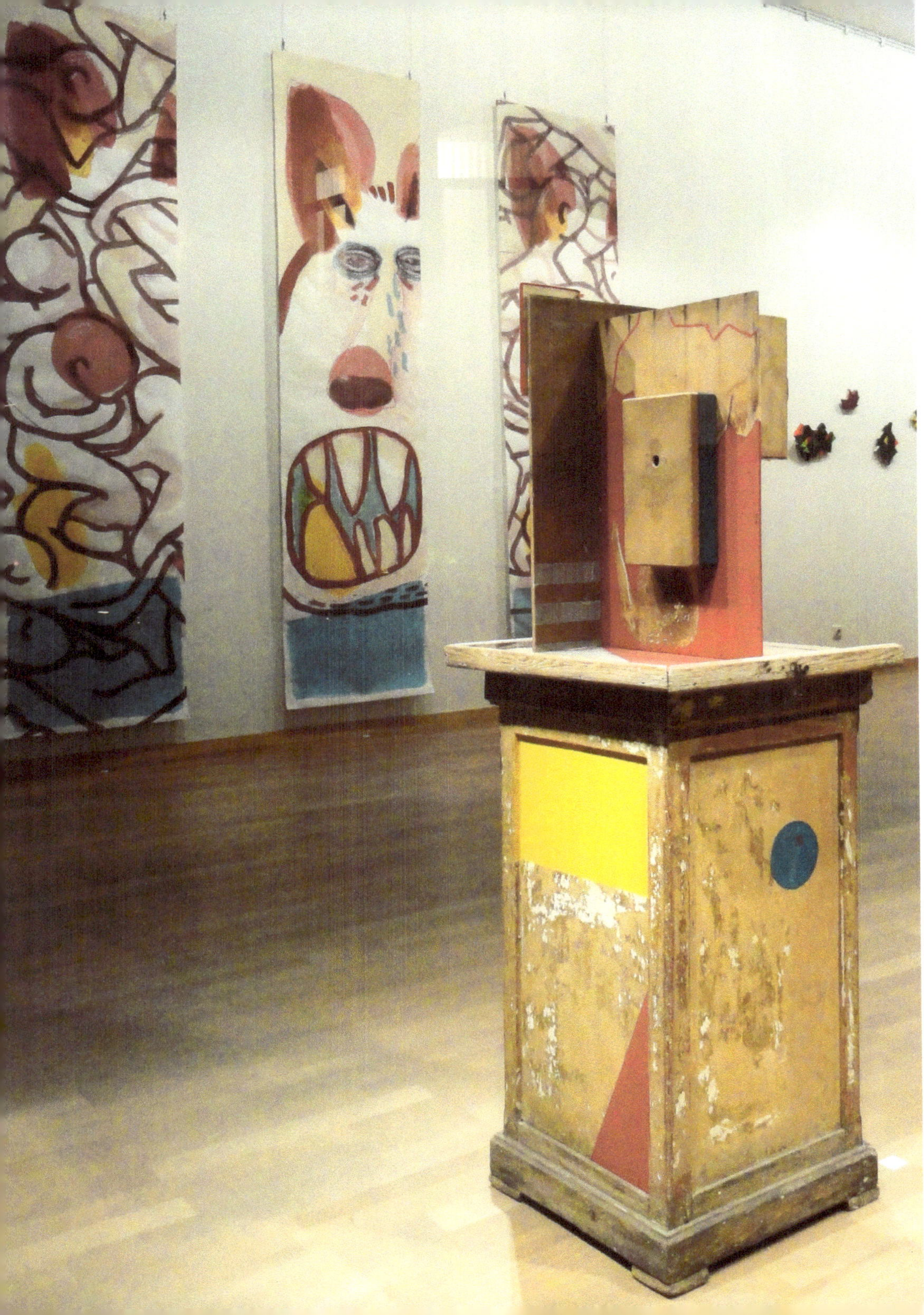

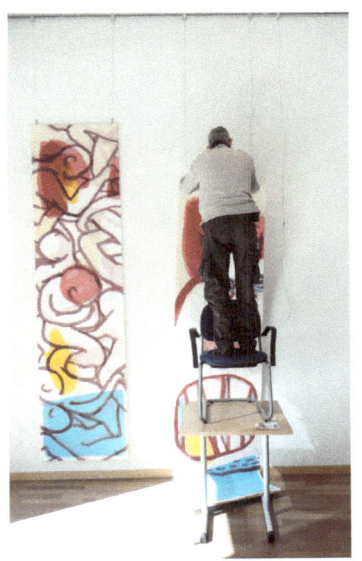

FABIAN
The novel Fabian by Erich Kästner as an installative Illustration
FACULTY of DESIGN, Münster 2011

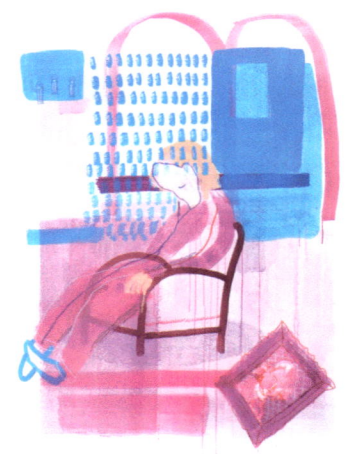
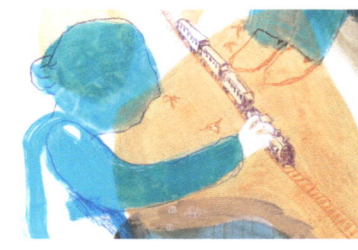

The golden twenties are gone, the brown thirties are about to come. Through telling the story of Dr. Fabian, Erich Kästners provides insight into the troubles and pleasures, loss of values and the new liberties in the final years of the Weimarer Republic.

Johannes Mundinger built a movable illustration, giving the chance to step inside his interpretation of the novel. The audience could move through the room in the room, listen to a soundcollage and 'feel' Mundingers view on the story of Fabian.

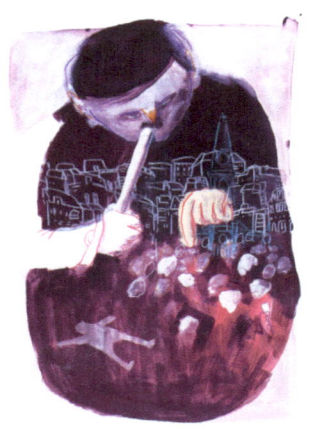
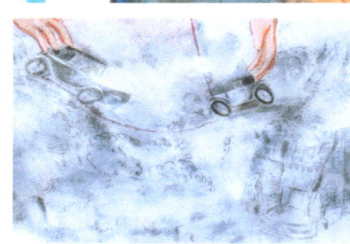
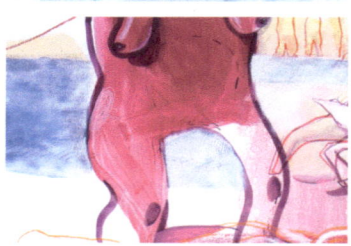

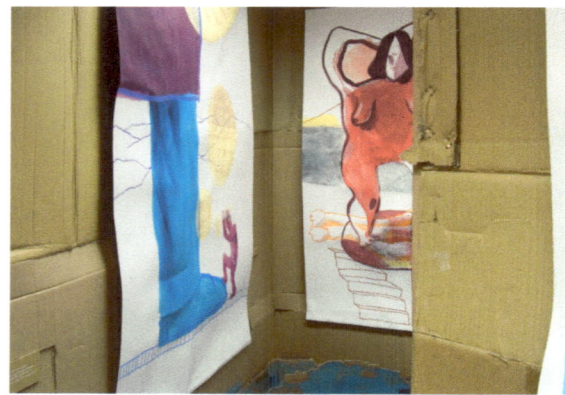
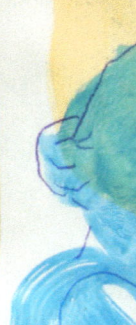

Photo by Malte Spindler

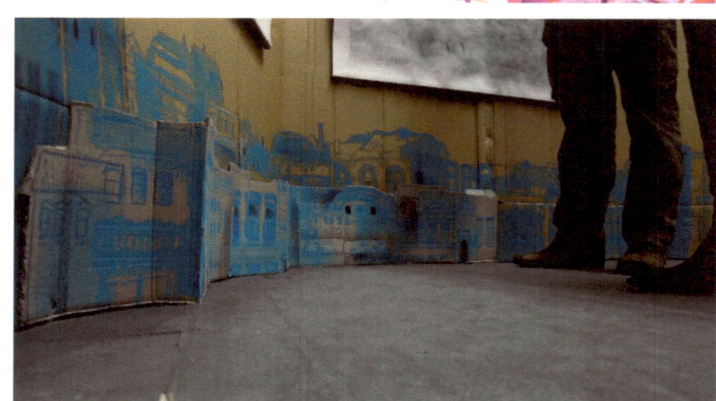

Photo by Malte Spindler

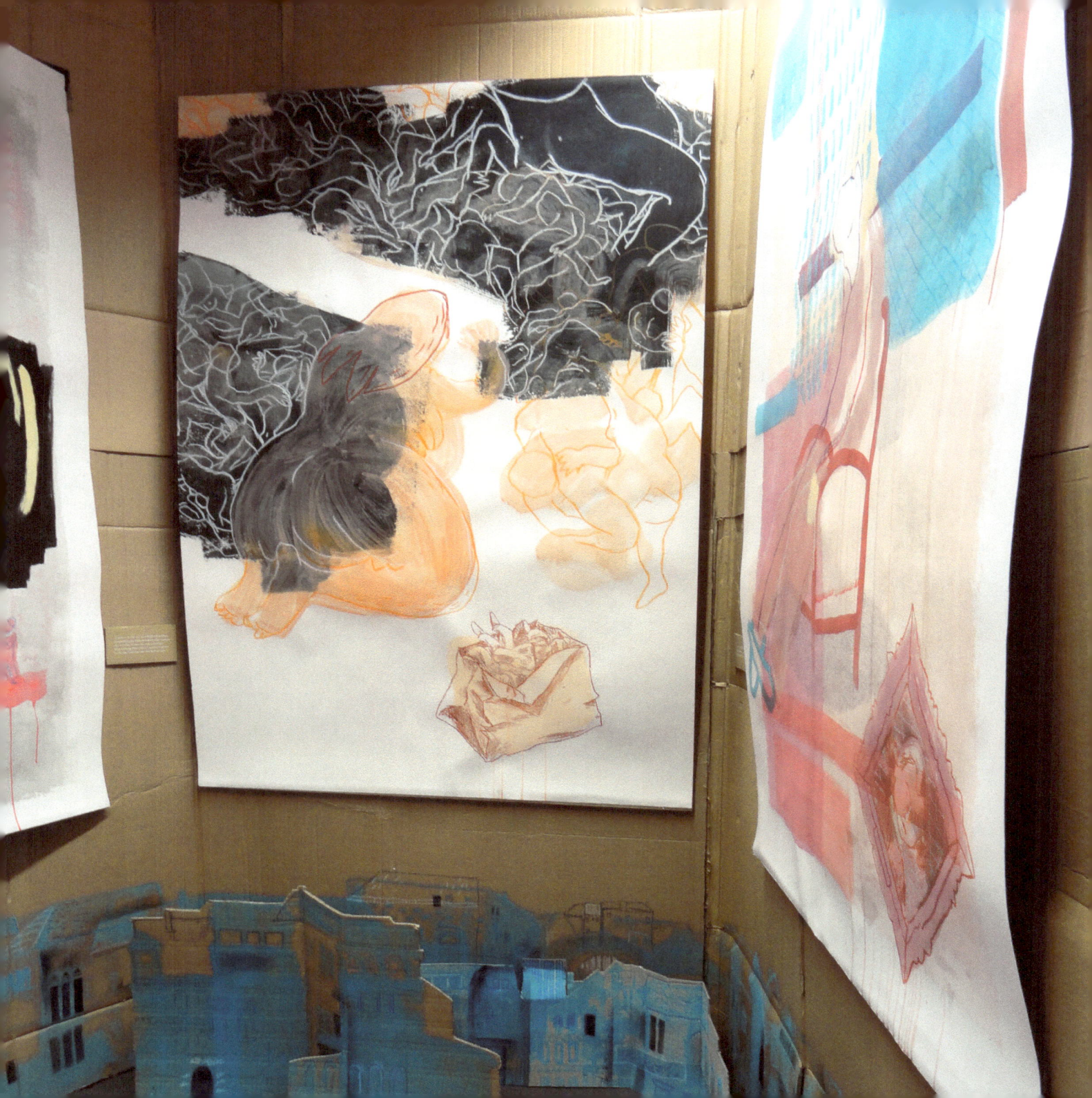

ZACUSCA

with Aitch, Dan Raul Pintea,
Saddo, Dirk Sandbaumhüter

TRIPTYCHON, Münster, 2011

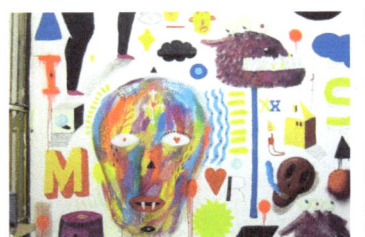 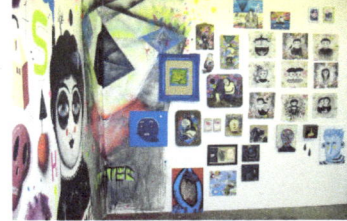 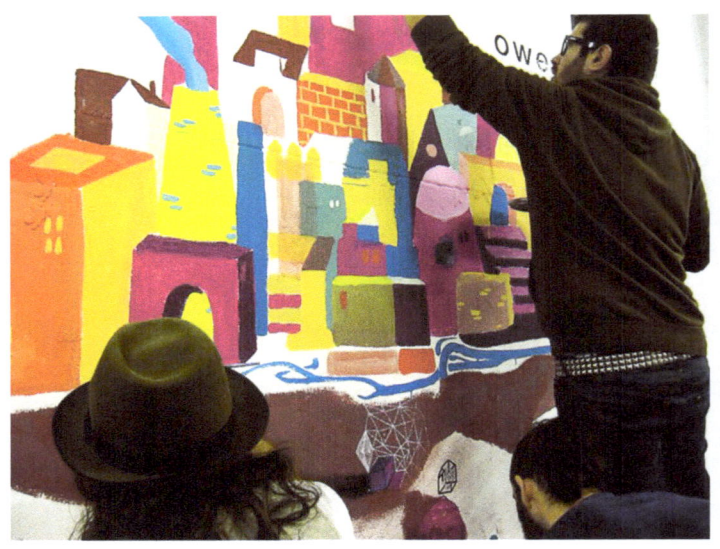

STICKER IN DER KUNST

Studienzentrum Museum Weserburg
Bremen, 2011/12

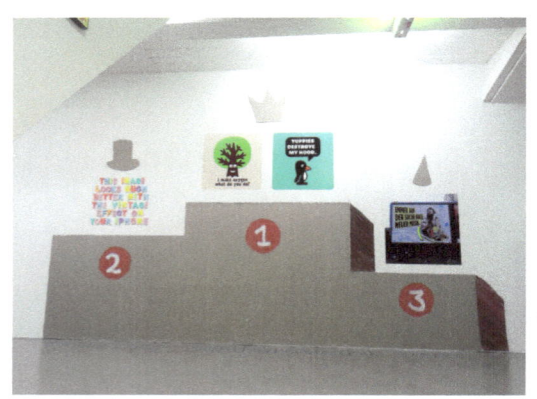 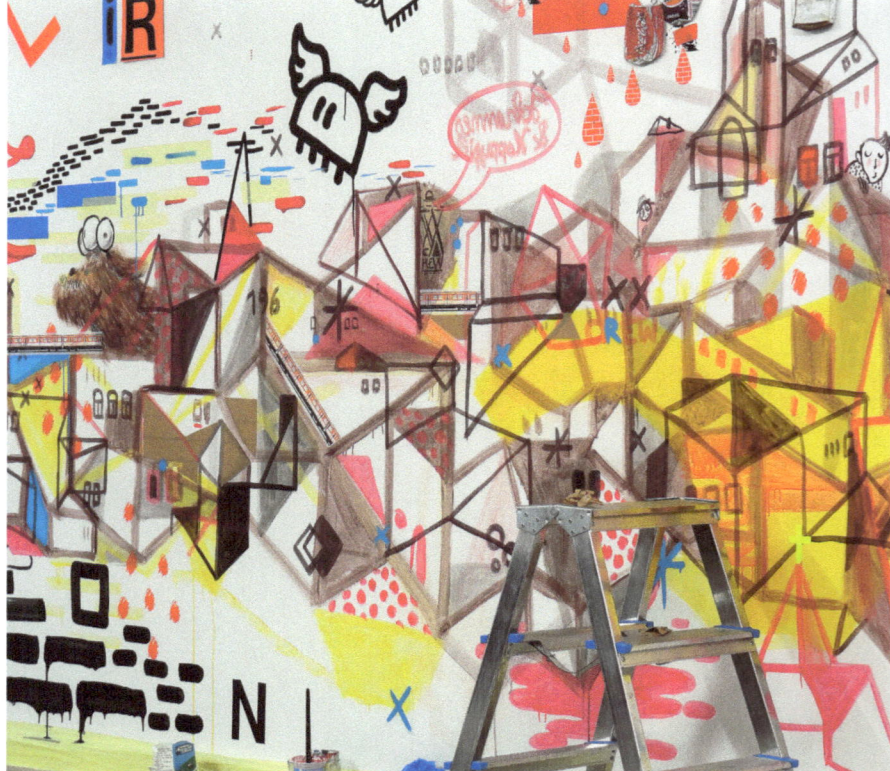

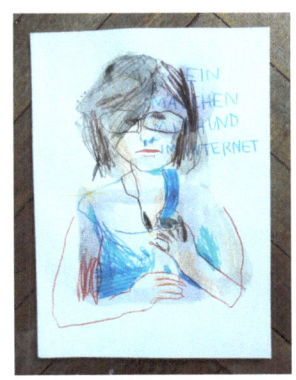
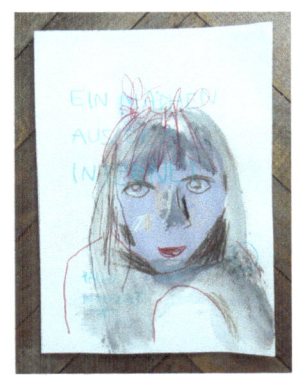
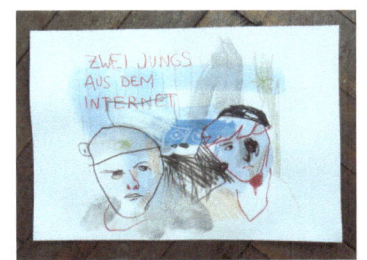
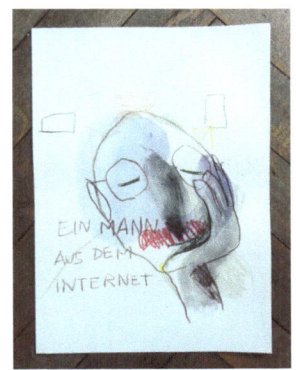

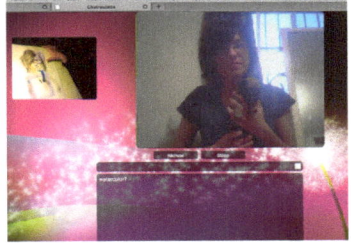
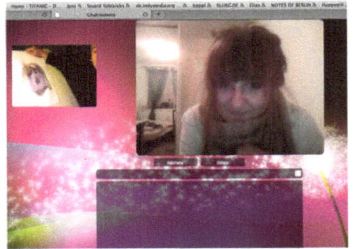
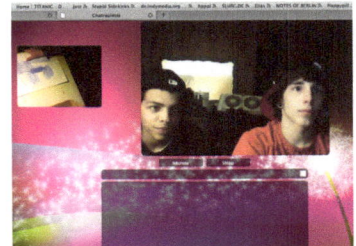
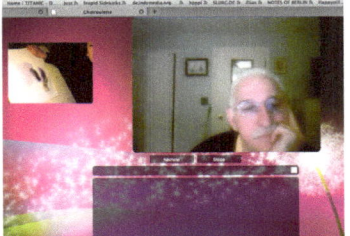

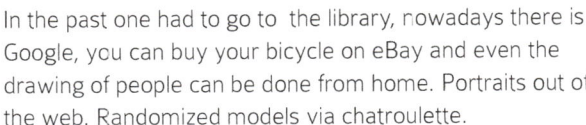

CHATROULETTE PORTRAITS
Berliner Kunstverein, Münster 2011

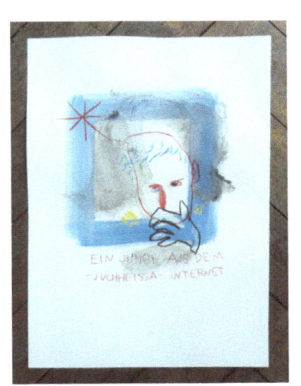
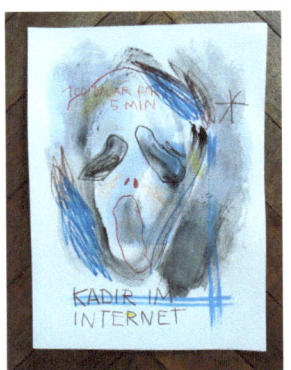

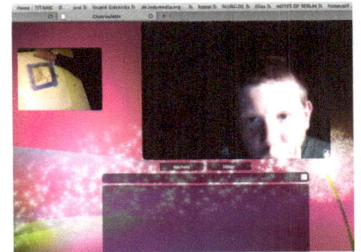
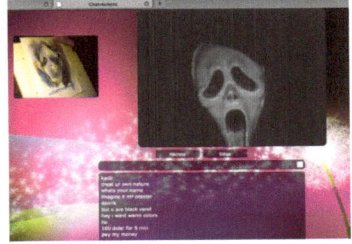

In the past one had to go to the library, nowadays there is Google, you can buy your bicycle on eBay and even the drawing of people can be done from home. Portraits out of the web. Randomized models via chatroulette.

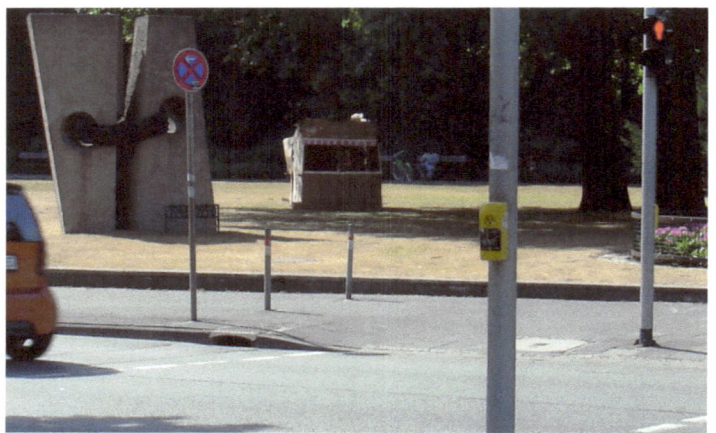

KIOSK

Bulky-waste-collaboration:
XX CREW feat. NARTUR Kunstgruppe

PUBLIC SPACE, Münster, 2011

MEETING of fART
Mein Hausberg
ATELIER ZUKUNFT, Mainz, 2010

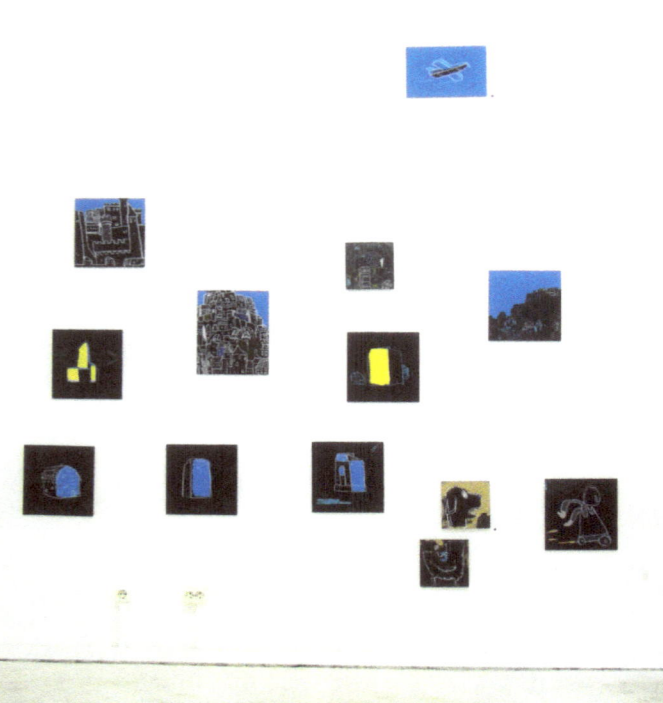

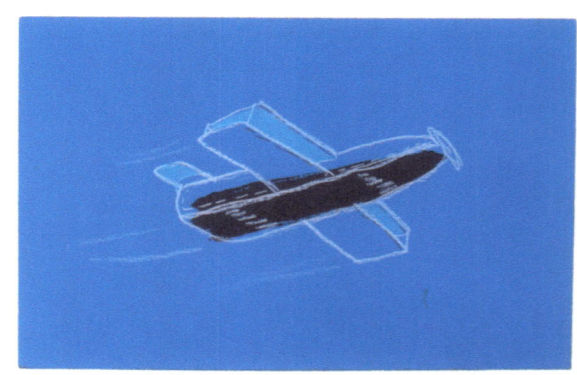

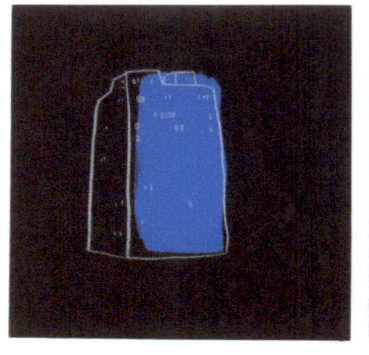

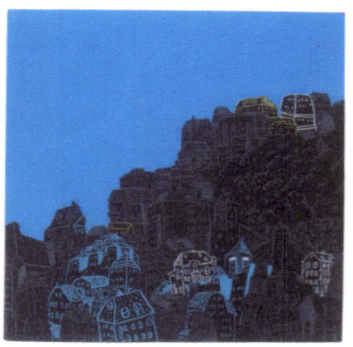

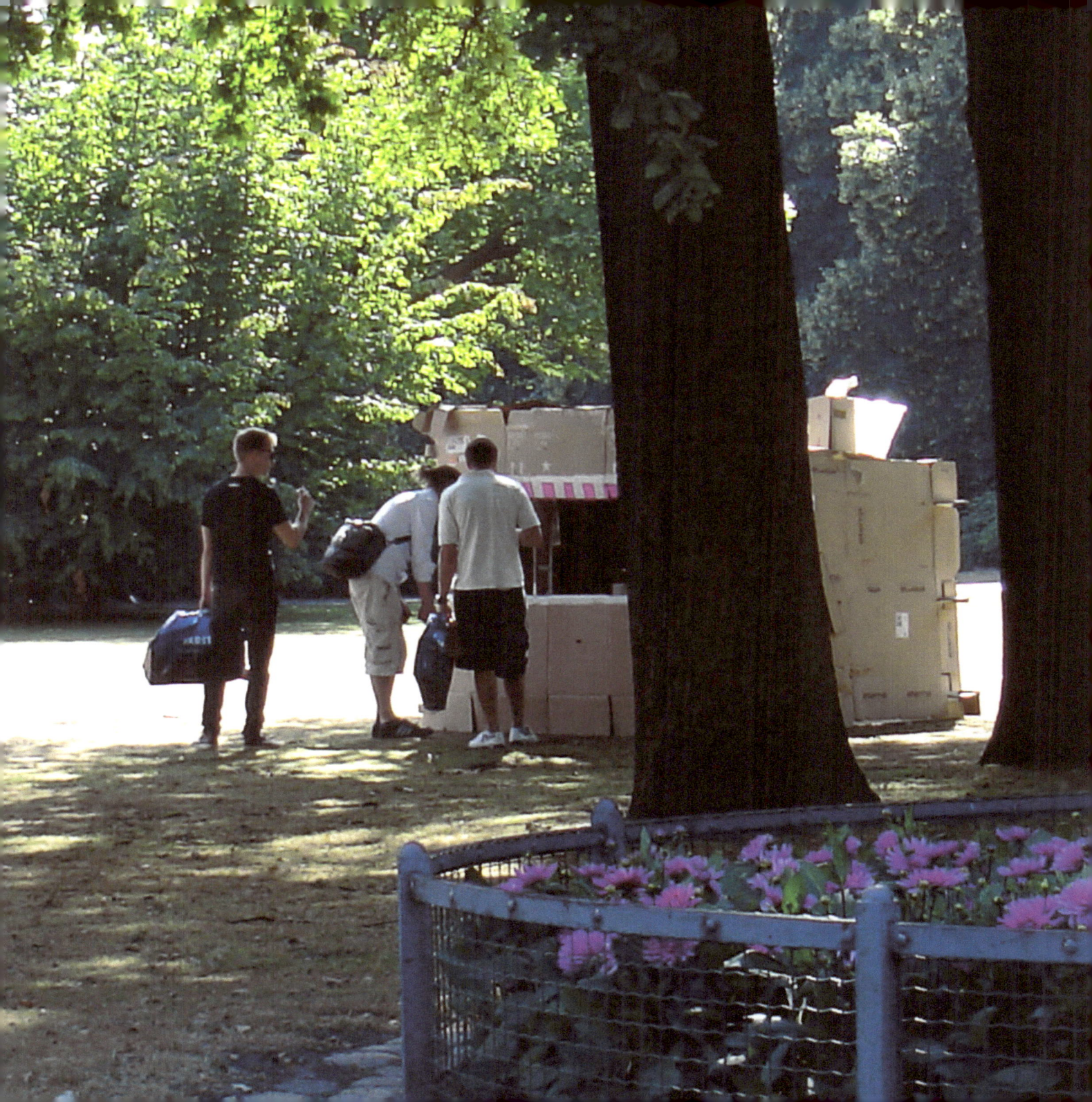

GALERIE KLOT
BERLIN

Gallery KLOT invites to exhibitions once every three months, curated by Johannes Mundinger. The focus is on urban-artists, figurative paintings, graphic arts and prints. Currently it is located in a former brothel in Charlottenburg, Berlin.

Artists so far:
Azione, Billo, Book, Elias Errerd, Fogeljunge, Gibbs Rosa, Irgh, Johannes Mundinger, John Reaktor, Hazard Hope, Lena Schall, Mike Friedrich, Moi, Otecki, Patu, Tom Brane, Tomasz Kobialka, Urkel, Zéh Palito, Volker#1, Zone

Musicians: Ellen Bonte, Jason & Theodor

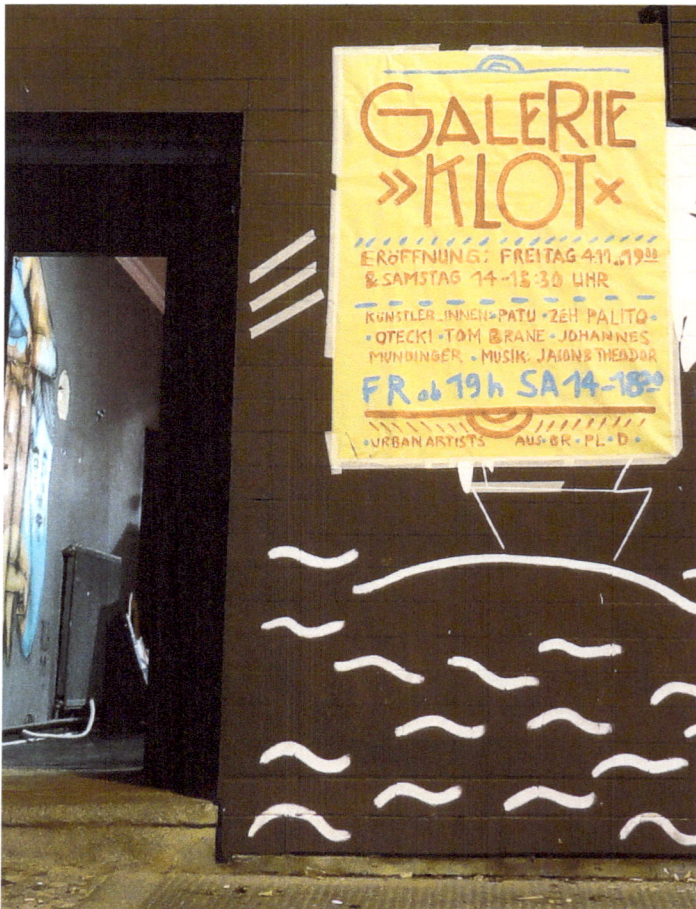

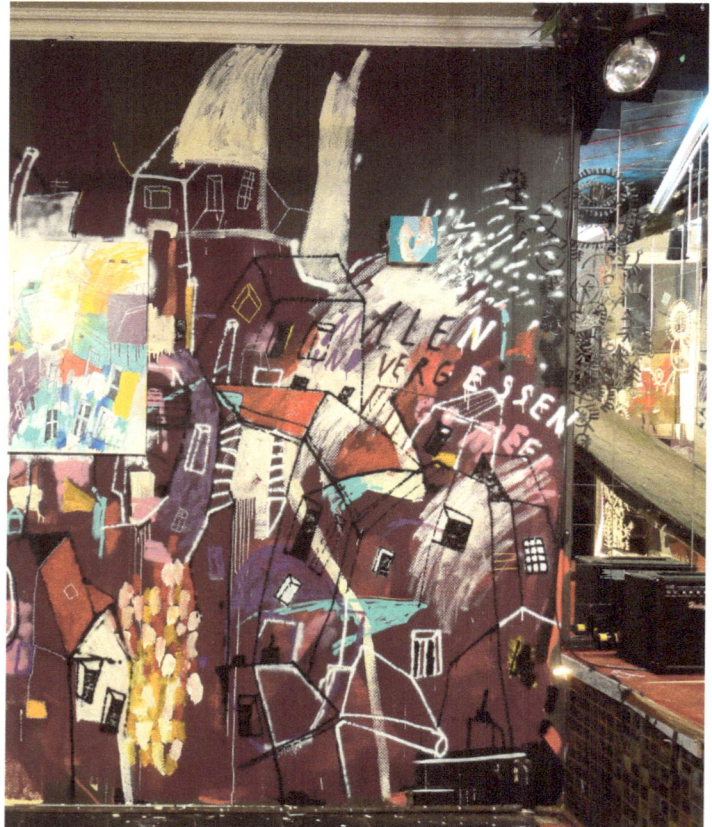

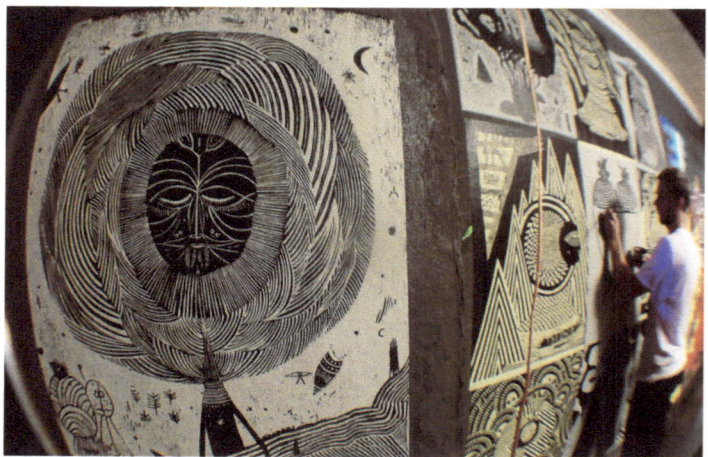

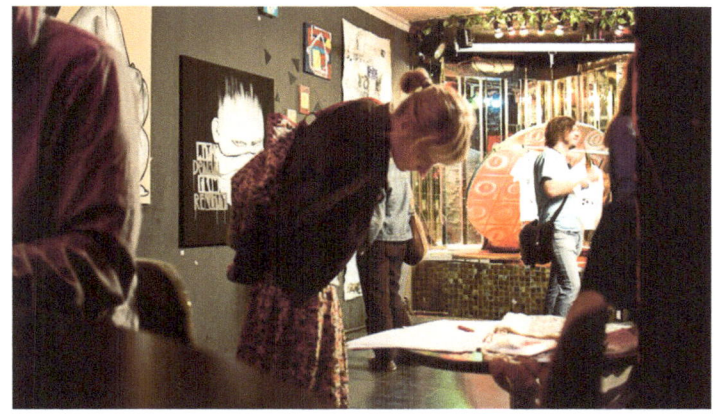
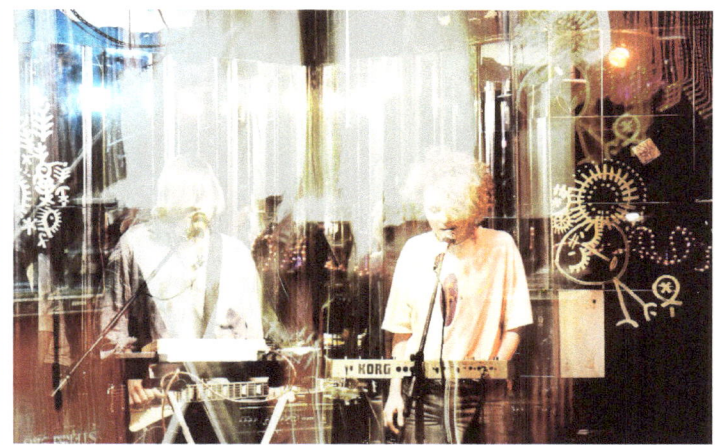
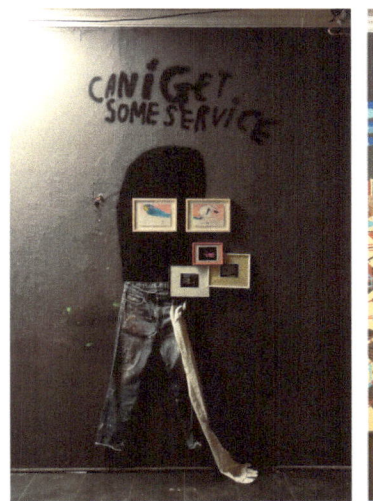
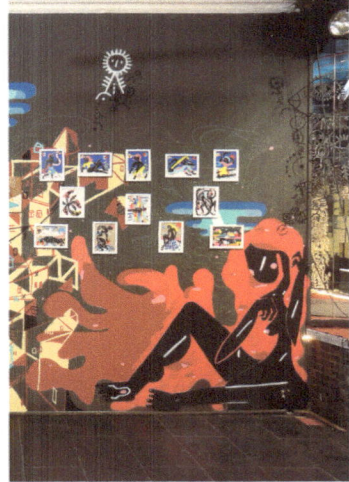
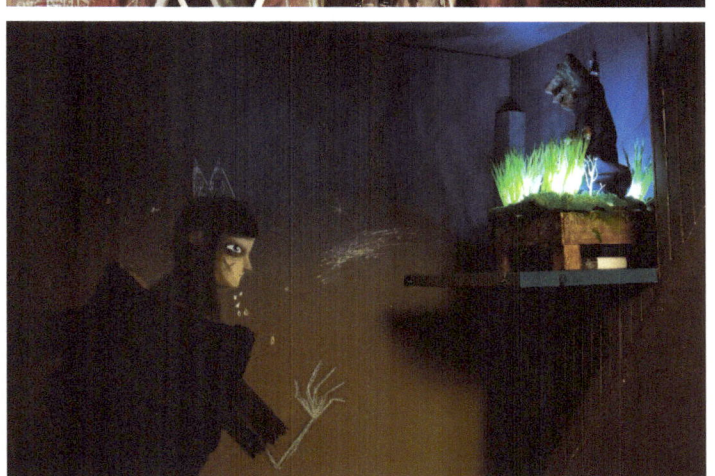
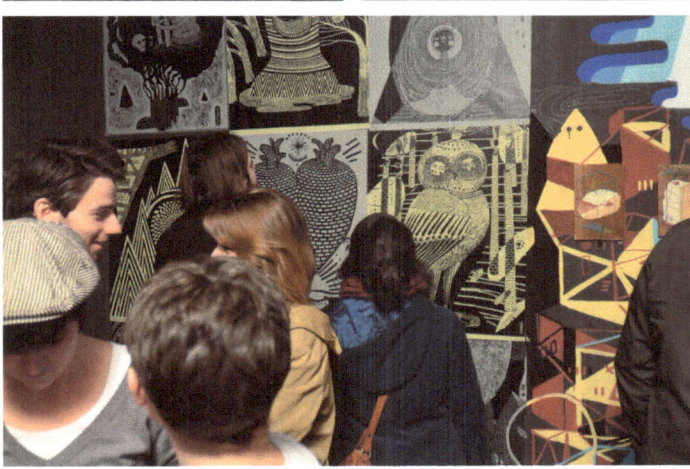
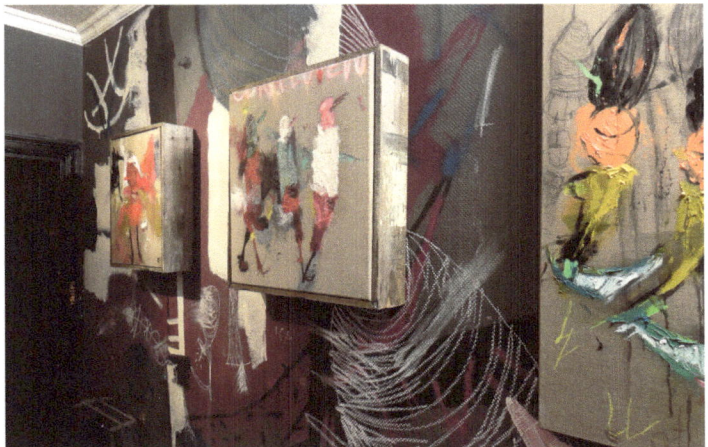

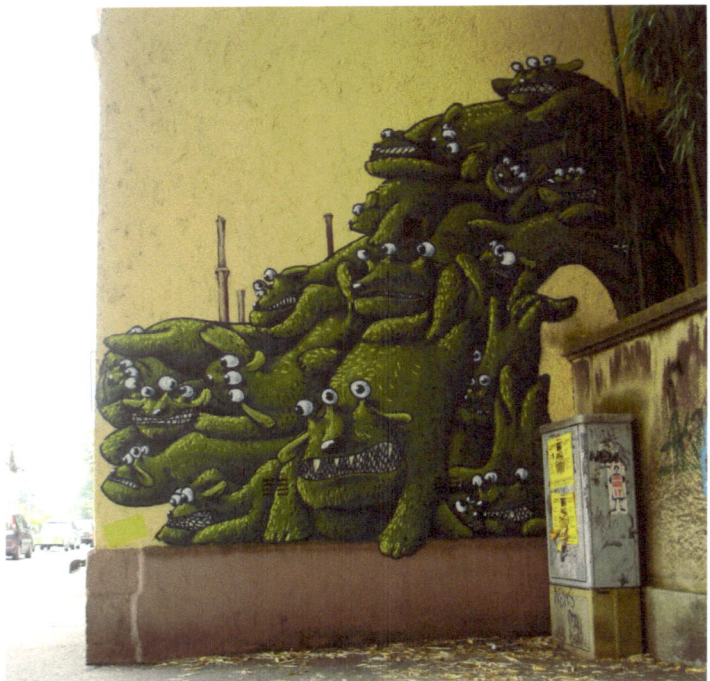

Offenburg, 2009

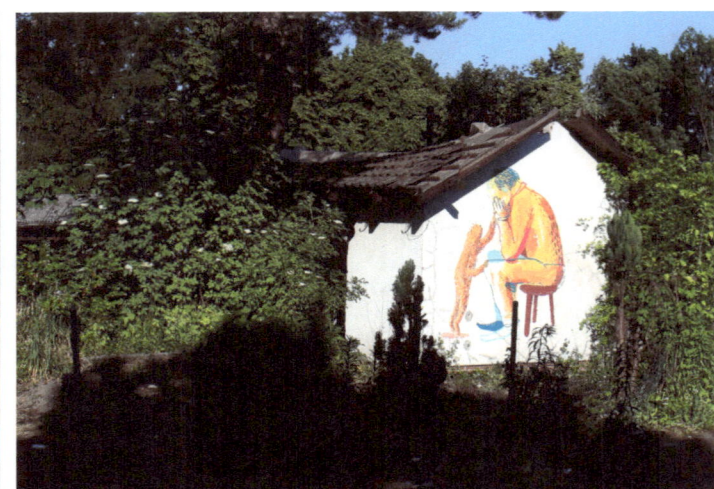

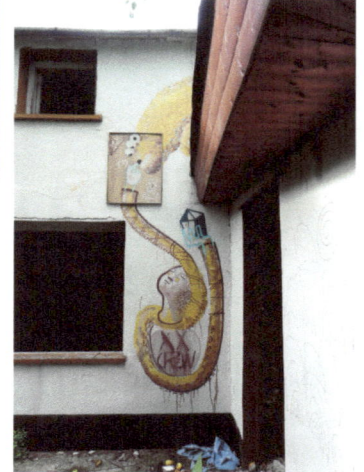

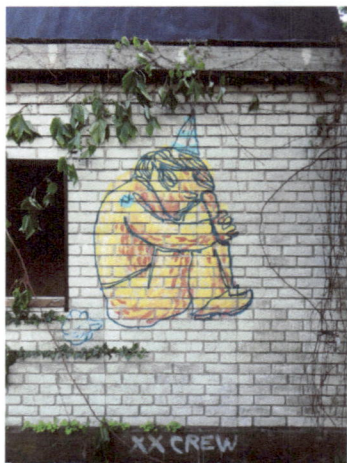

Berlin 2011

With Reab, Brussels 2011

Here a beautiful duo sharing a pillar. Reab from Bruxelles and Johannes (XX Crew) from Berlin. On the left we recognize Reab's style. He paints using the roller. A game of bars and curves finding their equilibrium à la American abstraction. On the right side: Johannes. Street artist and illustrator, his style reminds us of illustrations for children. The XX Crew has a very playful relation to urban art. "Our method is a child's game" is what they seem to be transmitting. The artist was visiting Bruxelles on the occasion of a painting journey.

Each time the pleasure consists in multiplying the experience. Here two universes face eachother (abstract facing figurative, simple and colorful versus naive and gentle) and the fresco works perfectly. Reab and Johannes belong to this new wave of painters, for whom the pleasure of creating outweighs the adrenaline rush of a clandestine practice.

Adrien Grimmeau, art historian

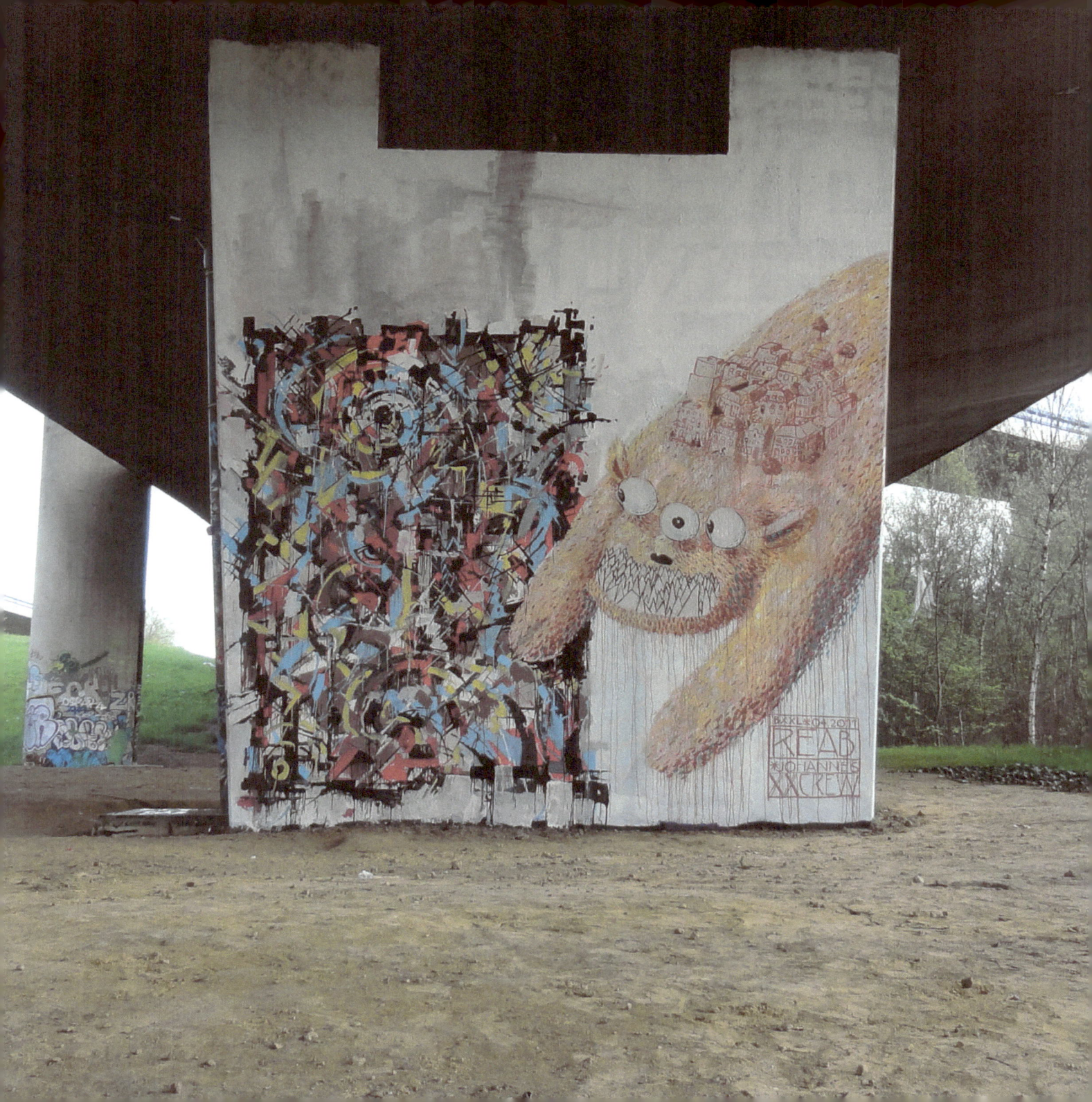

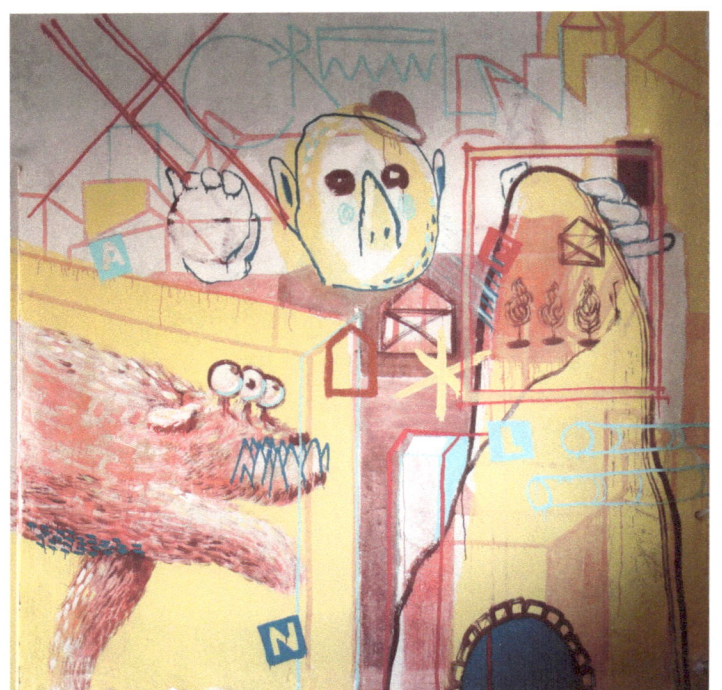

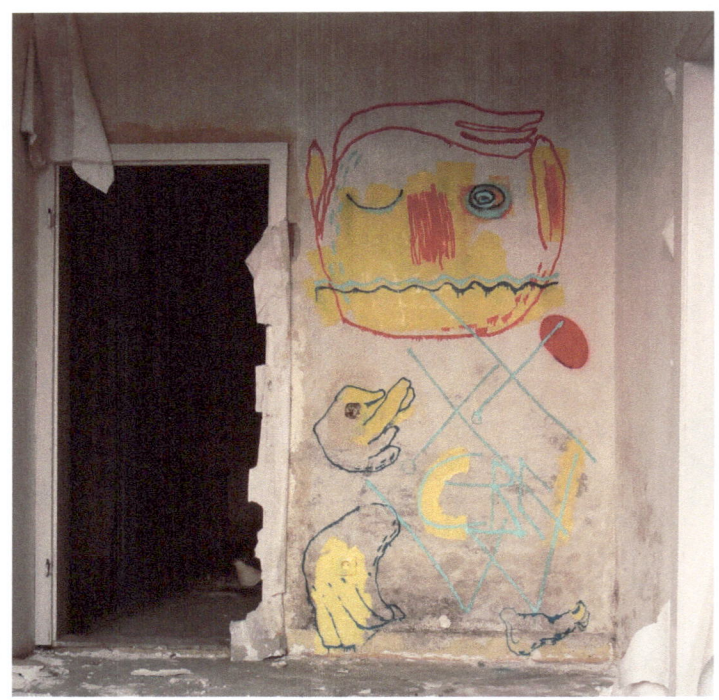

Berlin 2011

Airplane by Lena Schall

Opposite:
with John Rekator,
Sam Crew

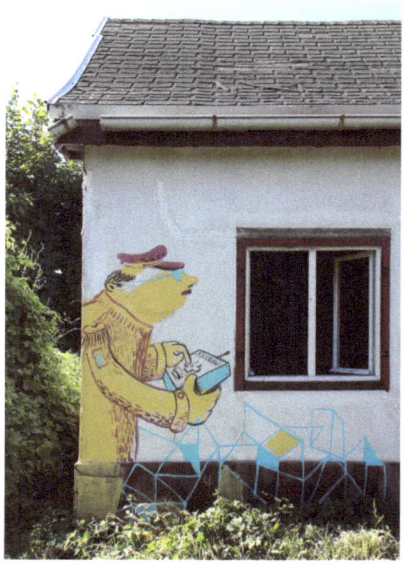

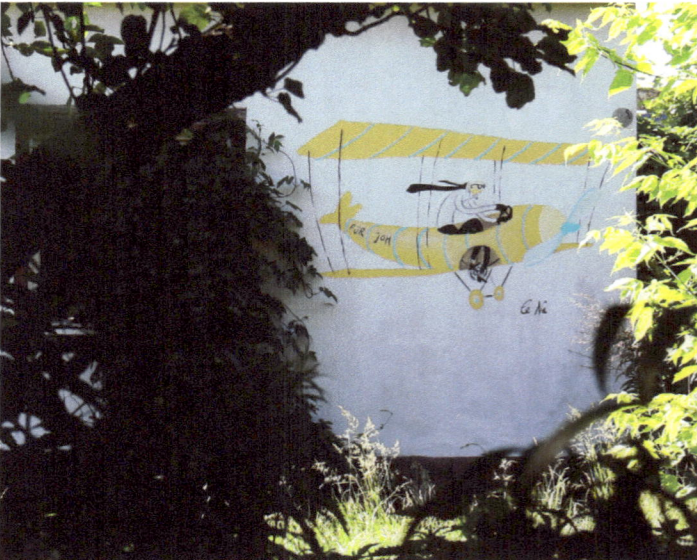

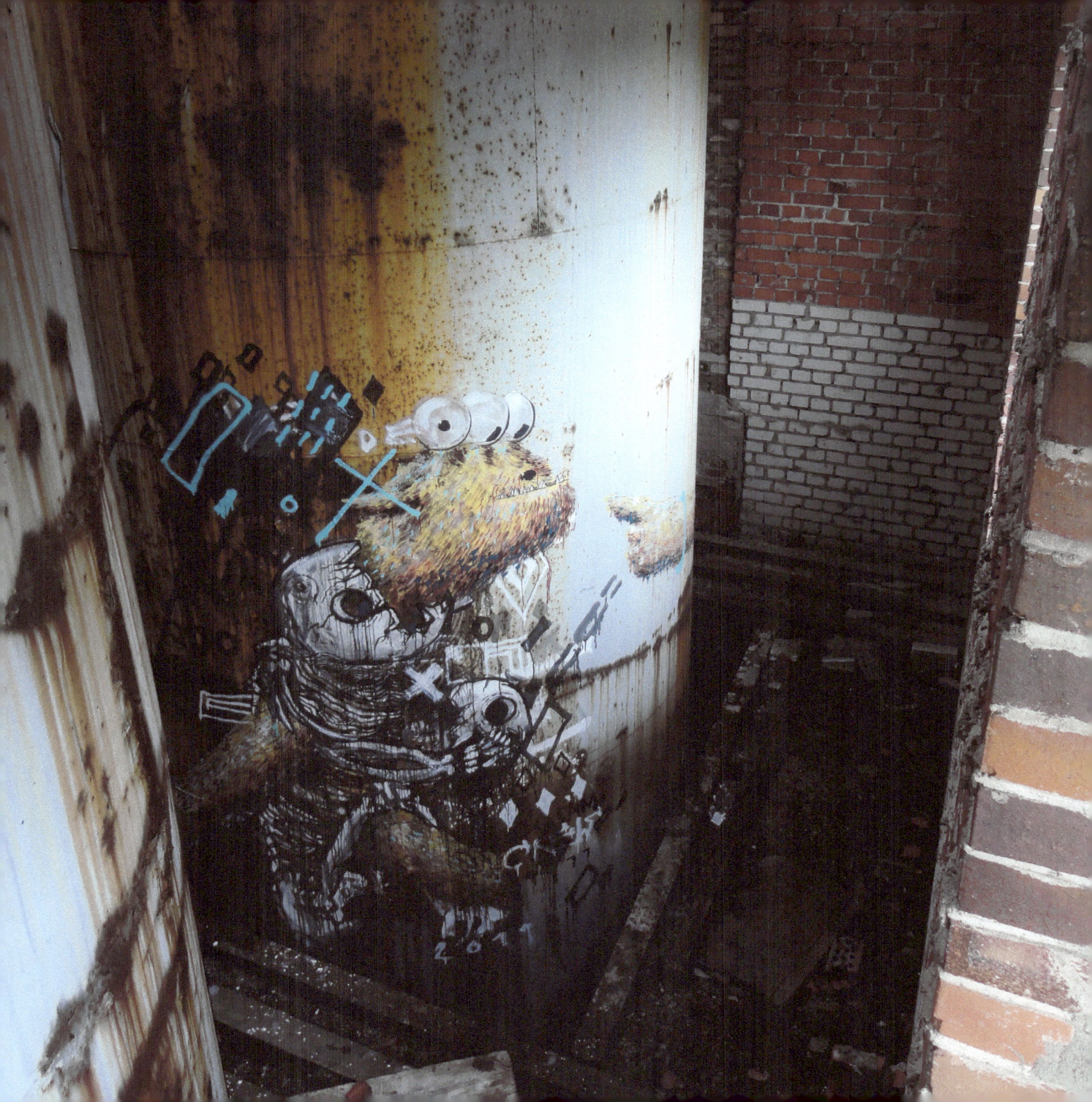

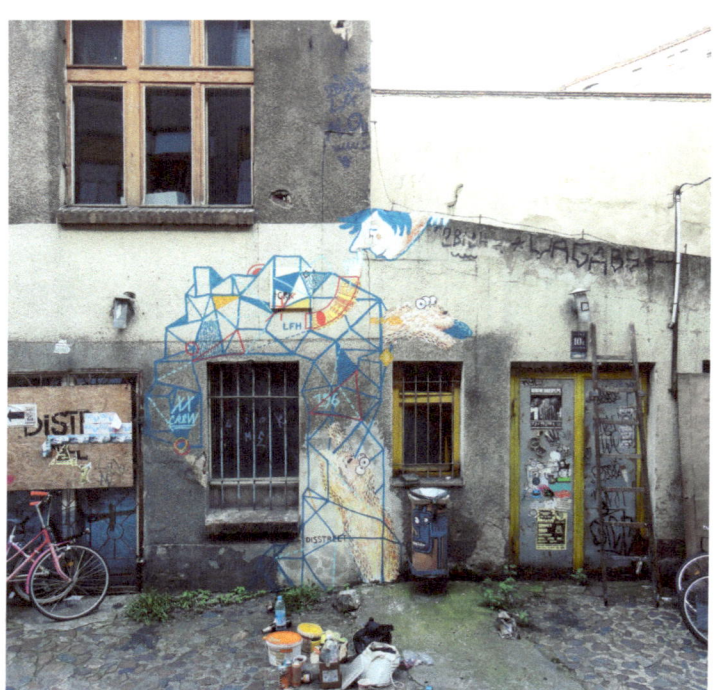

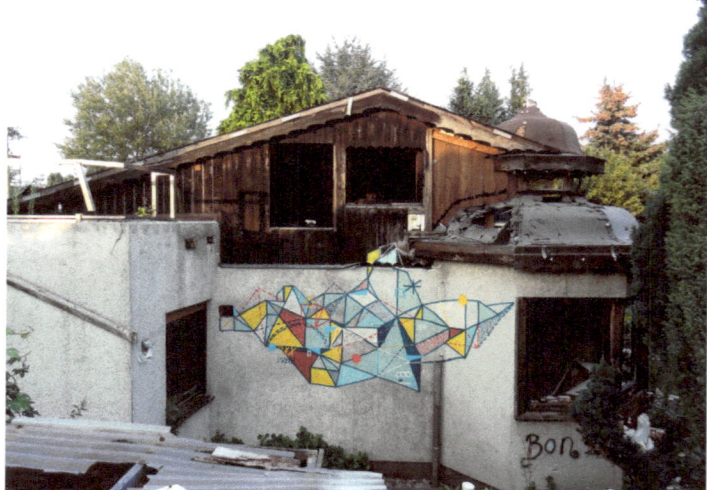

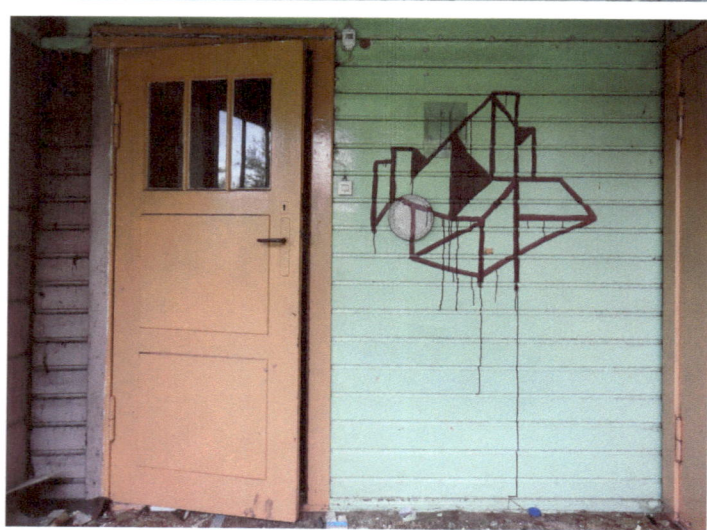

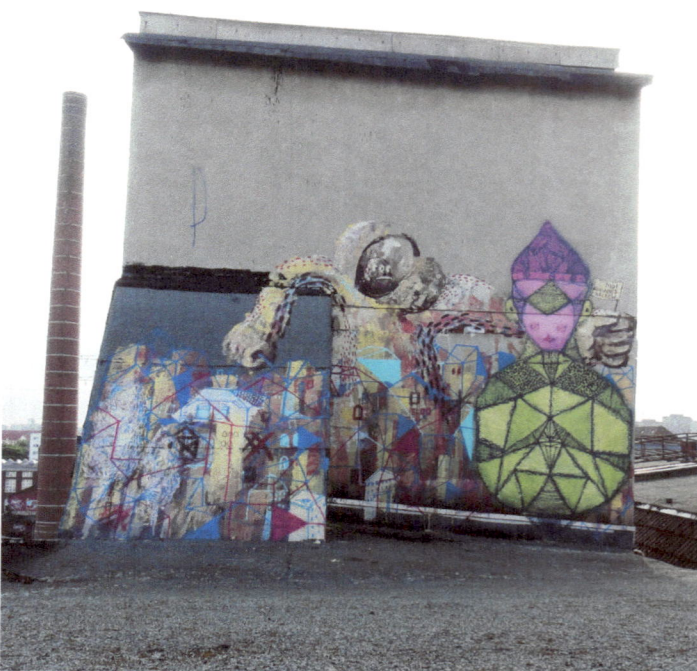

Wroclaw / Berlin 2011
Bottom right: with Moi /Nonstop Nonsens, Berlin, 2011

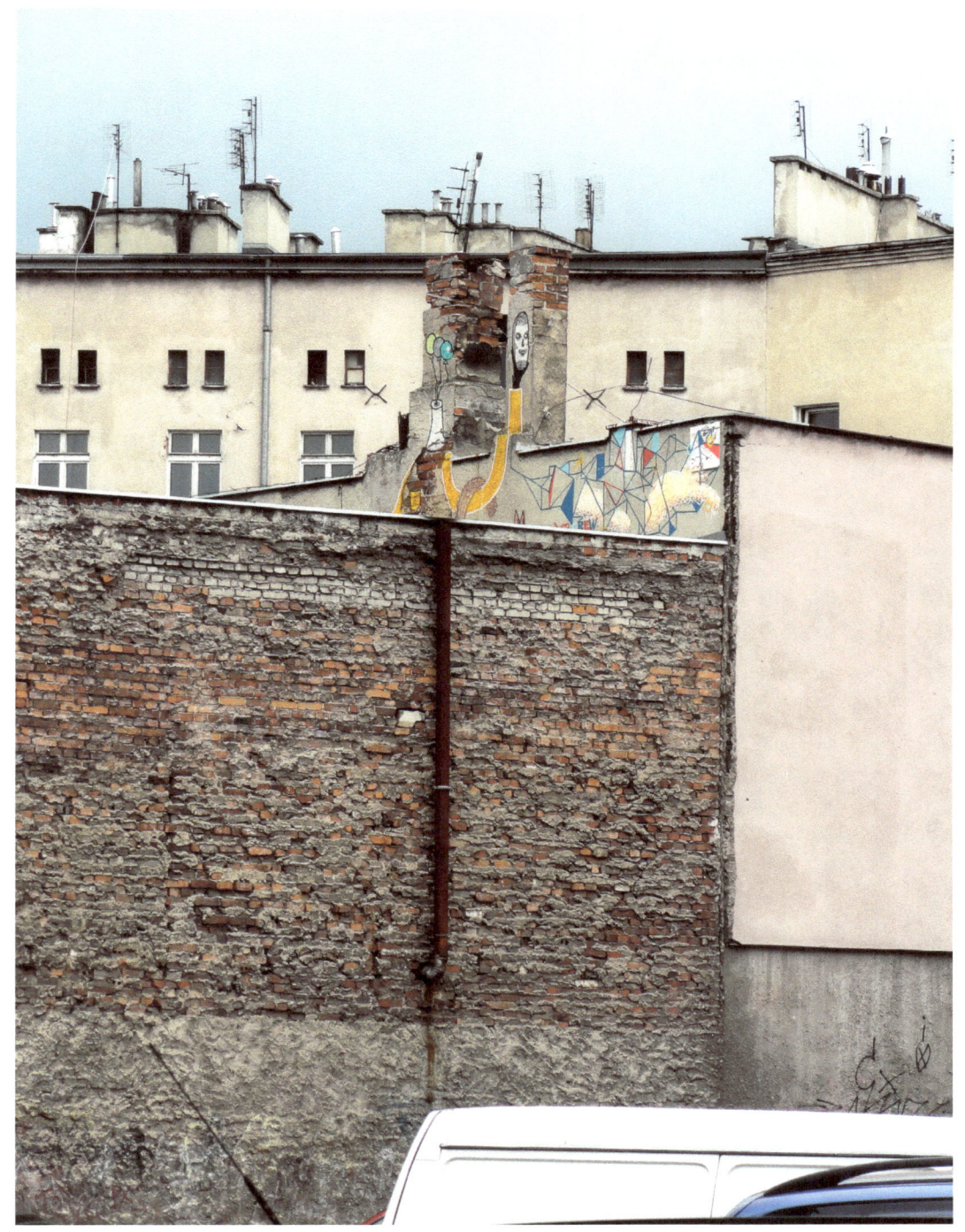

With Patu
CRK, Wrocław 2011

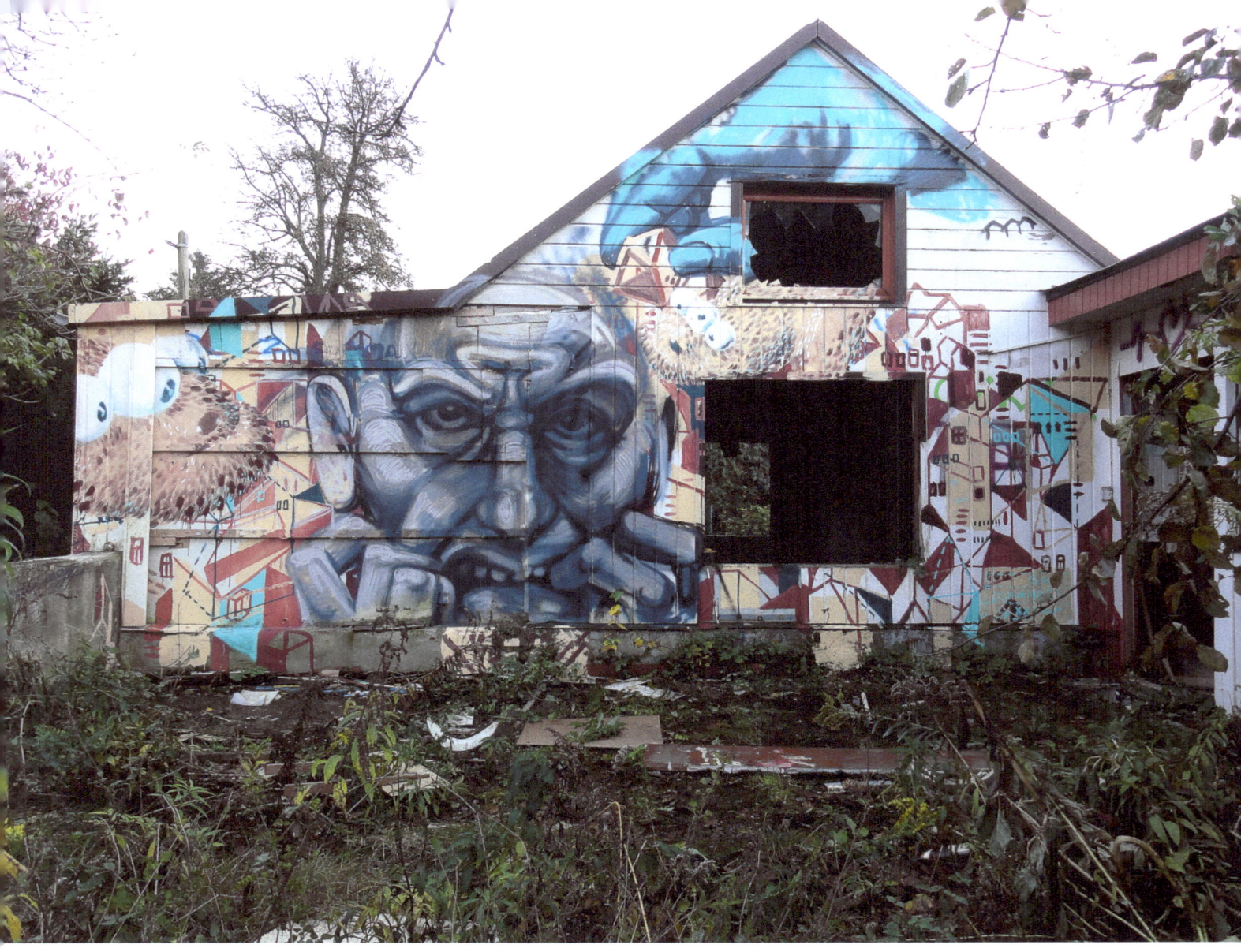

With Gaia, Berlin 2011
With Duncan Passmore and Tomasz Kobialka, Görlitz 2011

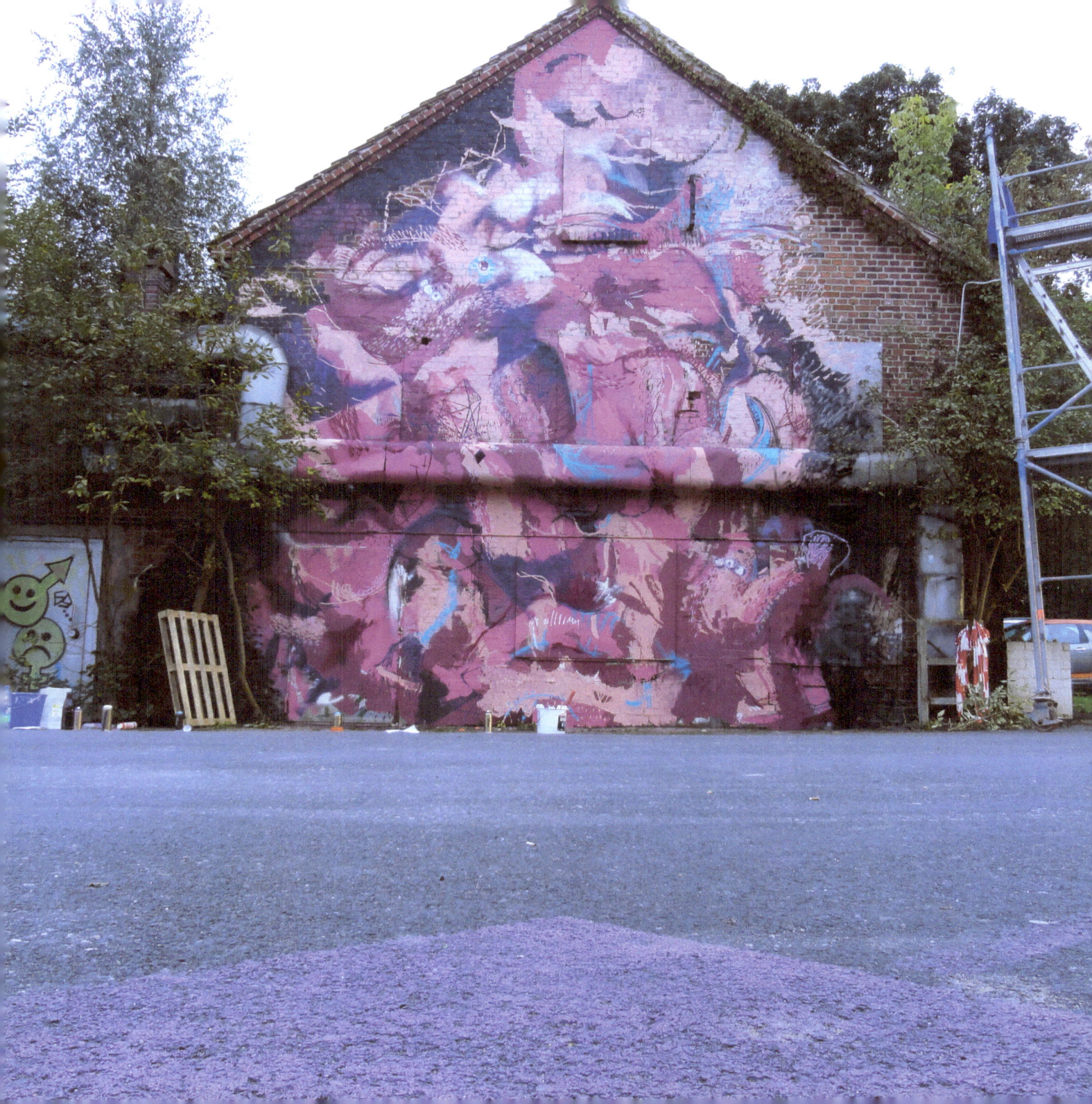

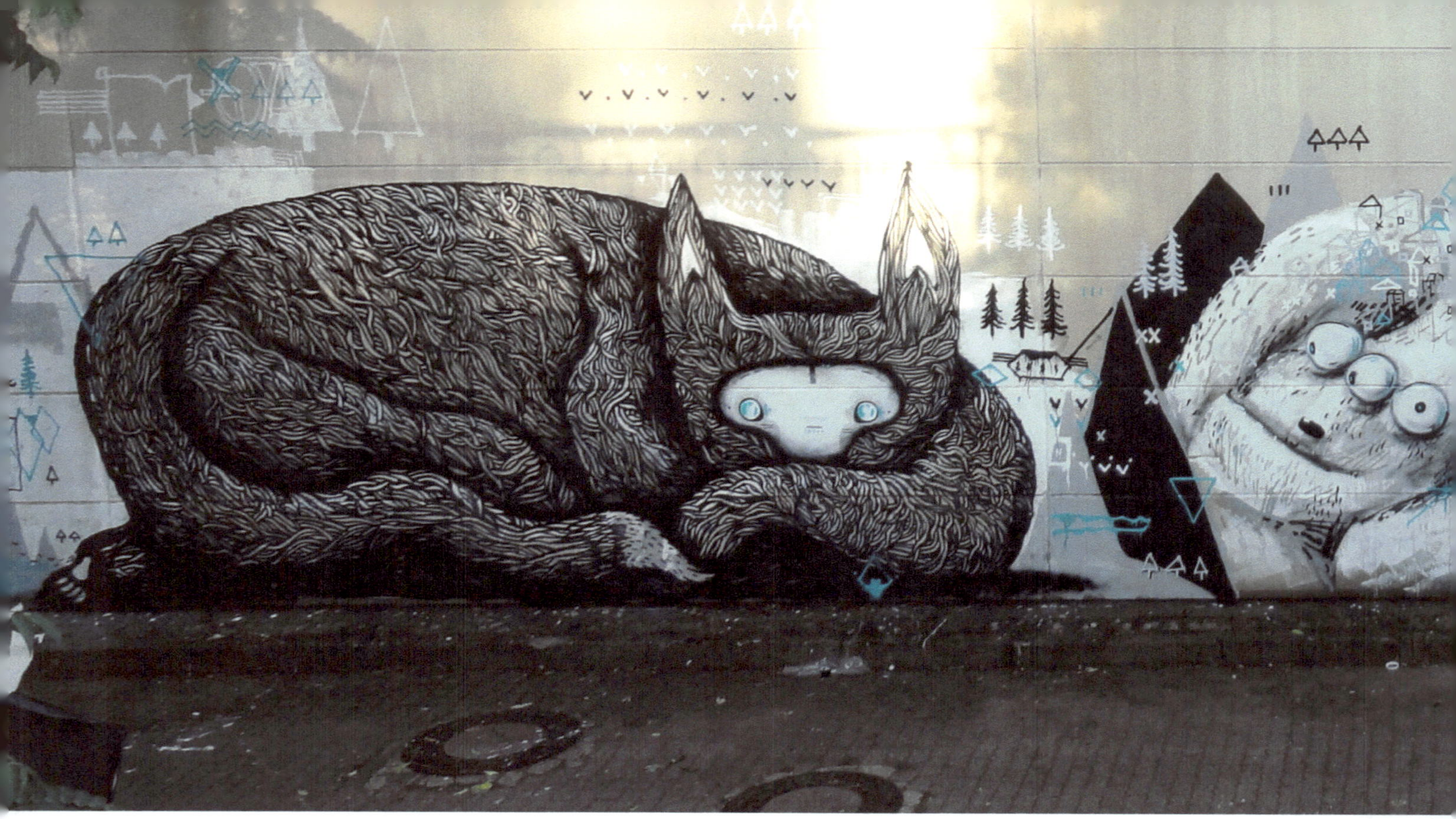

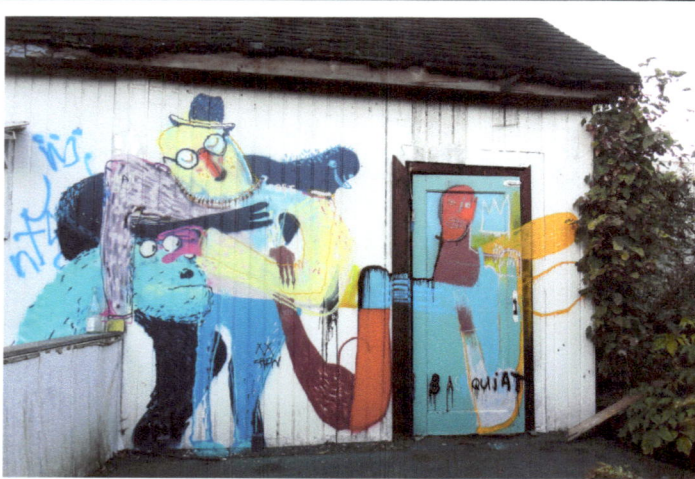

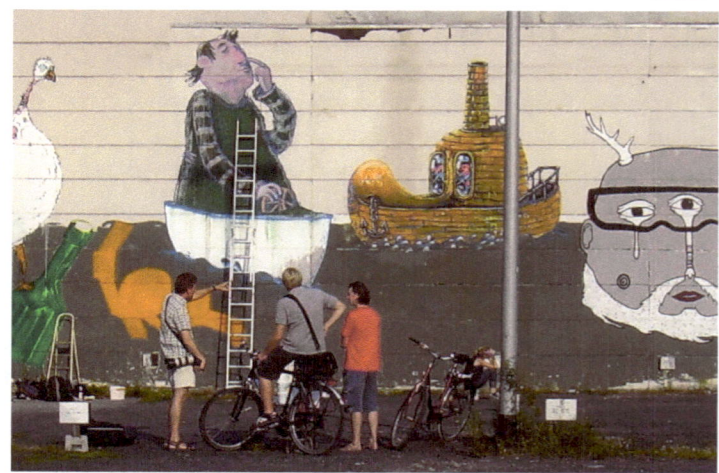

With John Reaktor /SamCrew, Irgh /Wurstbande, Moi /Nonstop Nonsens Berlin 2011
With Danny Gretscher, Berlin 2011 / Stupid Sidekicks & Wurstbande Collaboration, Münster 2010

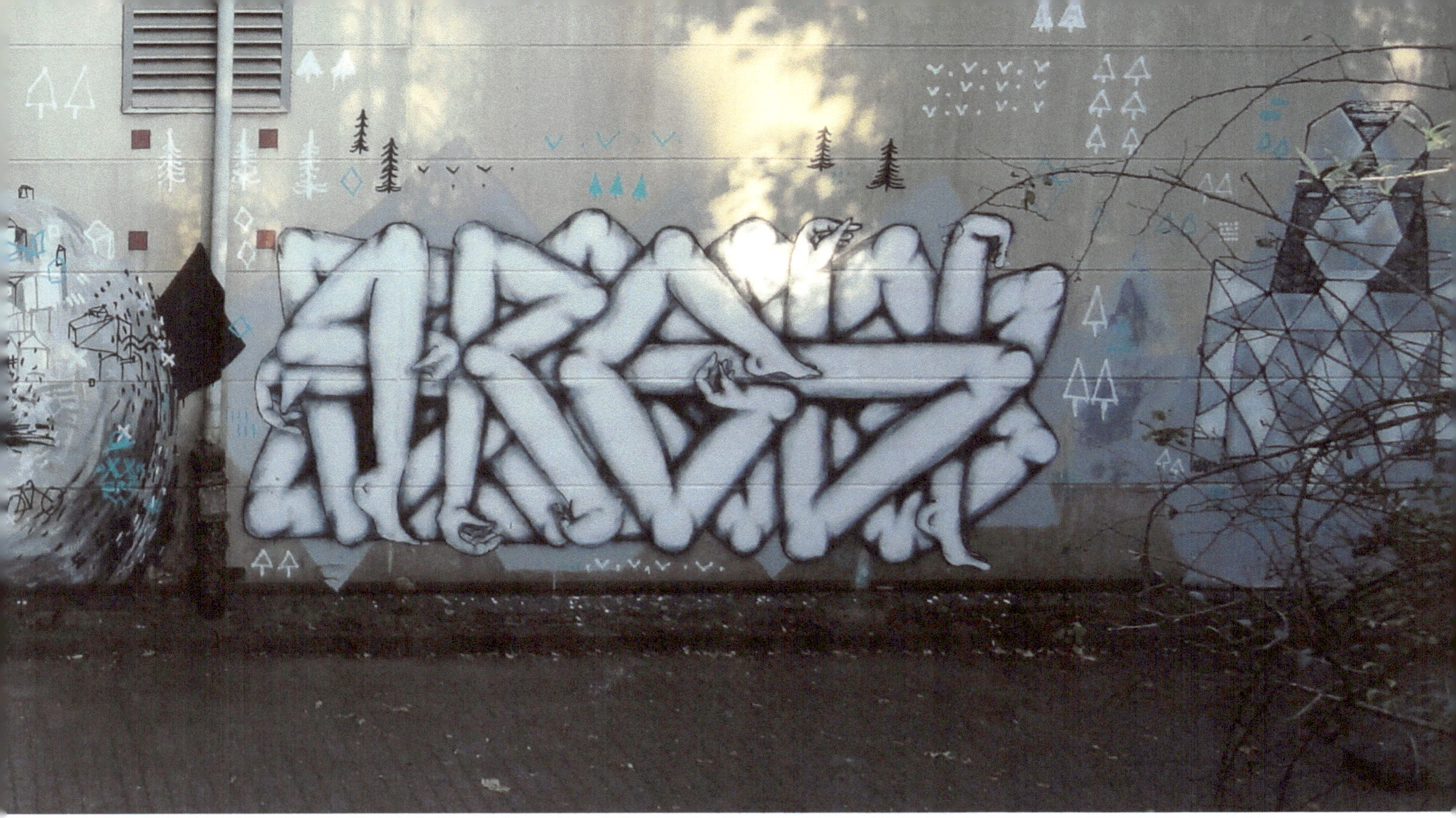

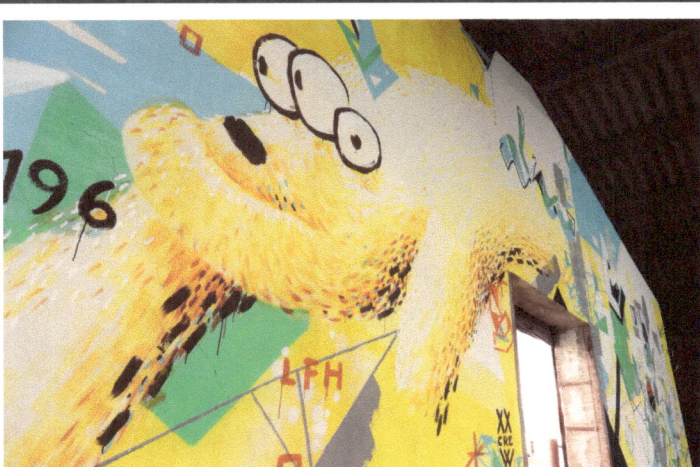
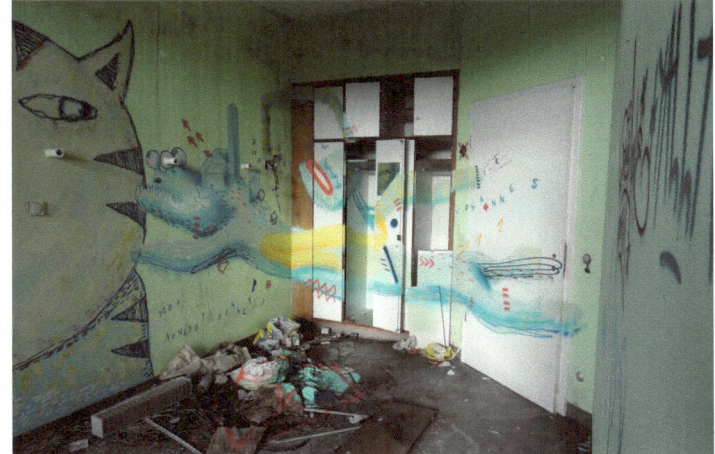

With Elias Errerd, Bruchsal 2011 / With Moi, Nonstop Nonsens, Berlin 2011

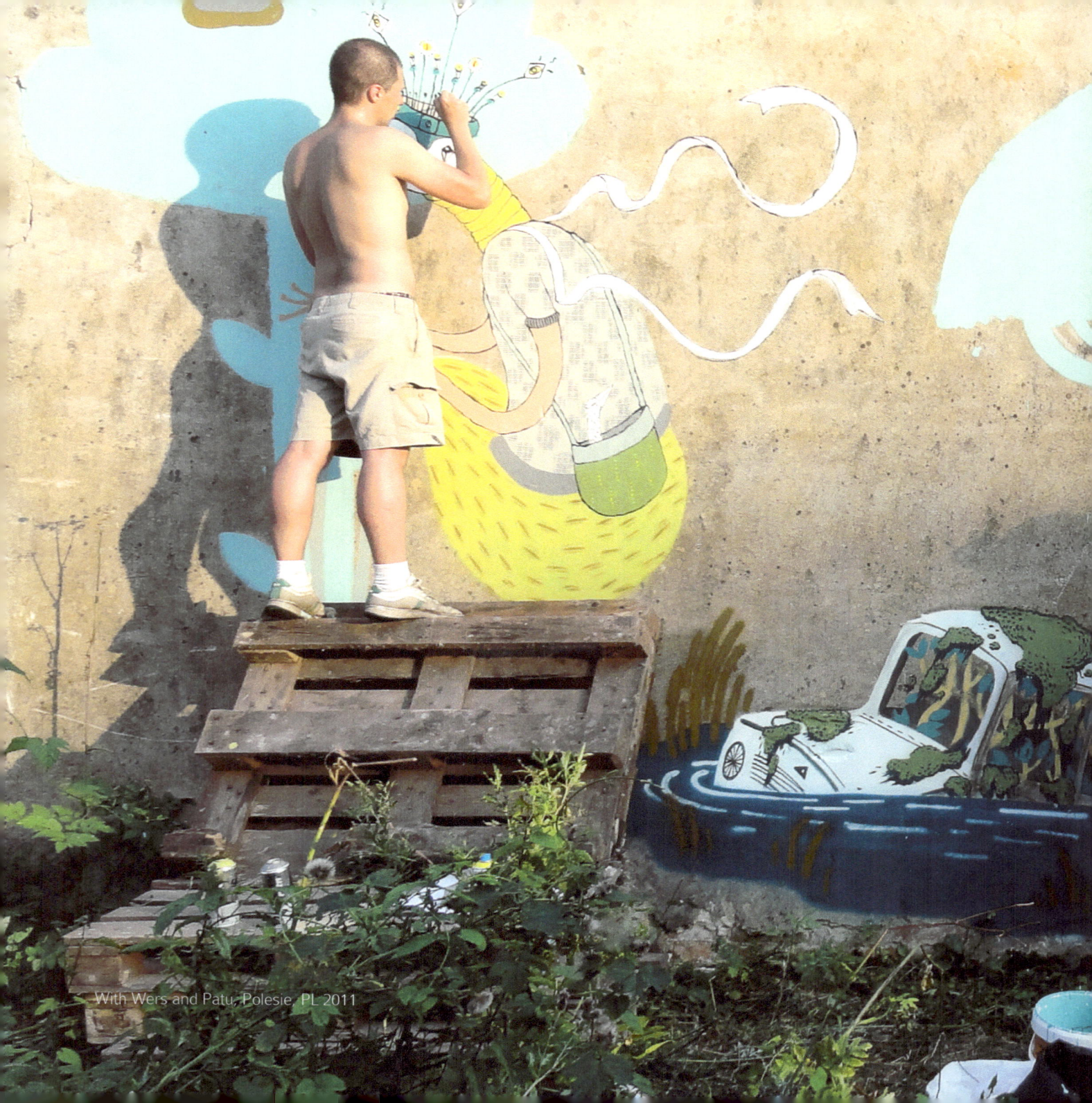

With Wers and Patu, Polesie PL 2011

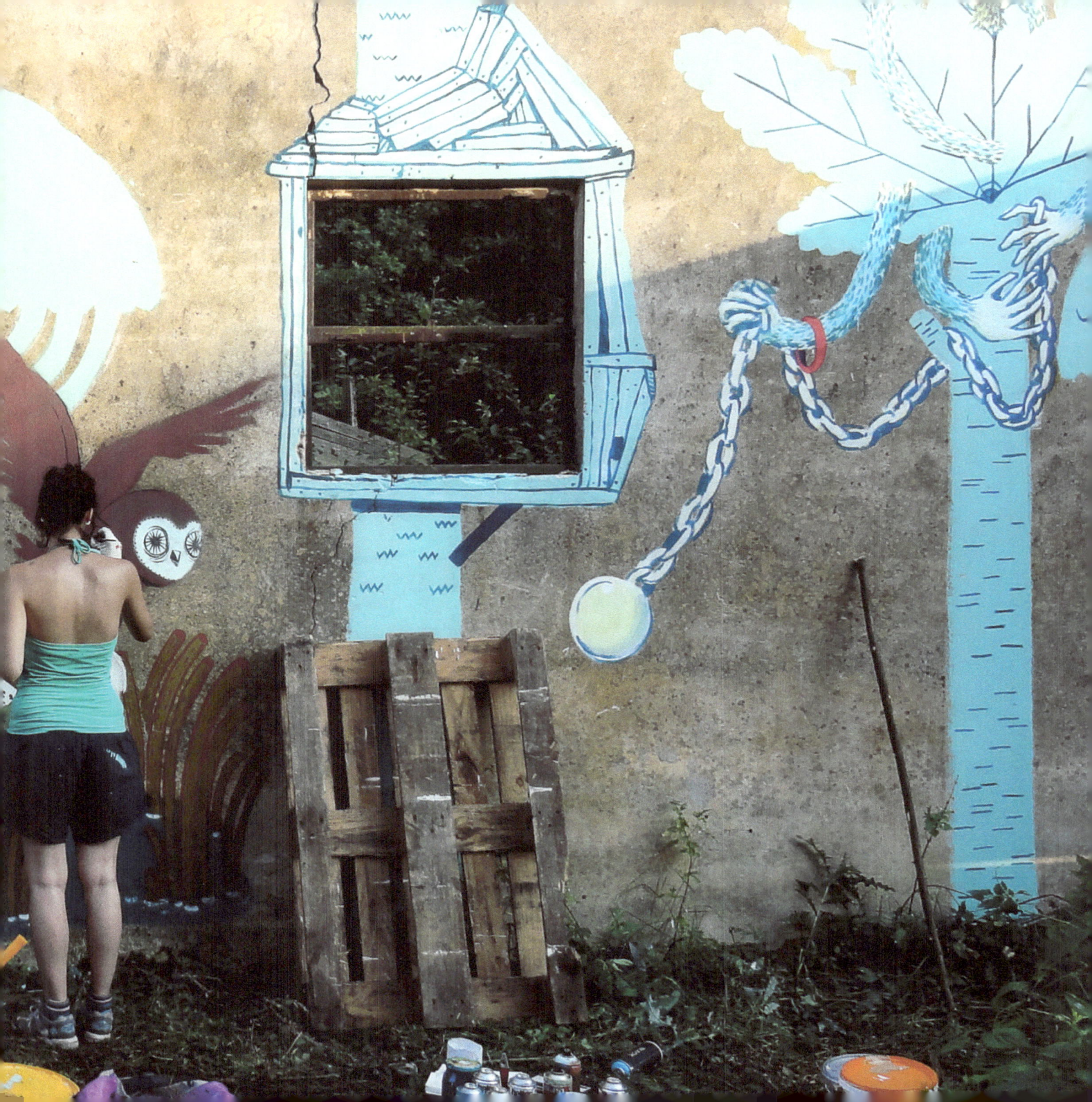

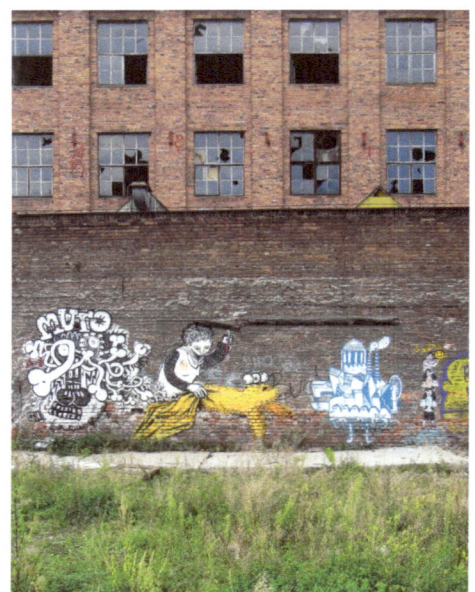
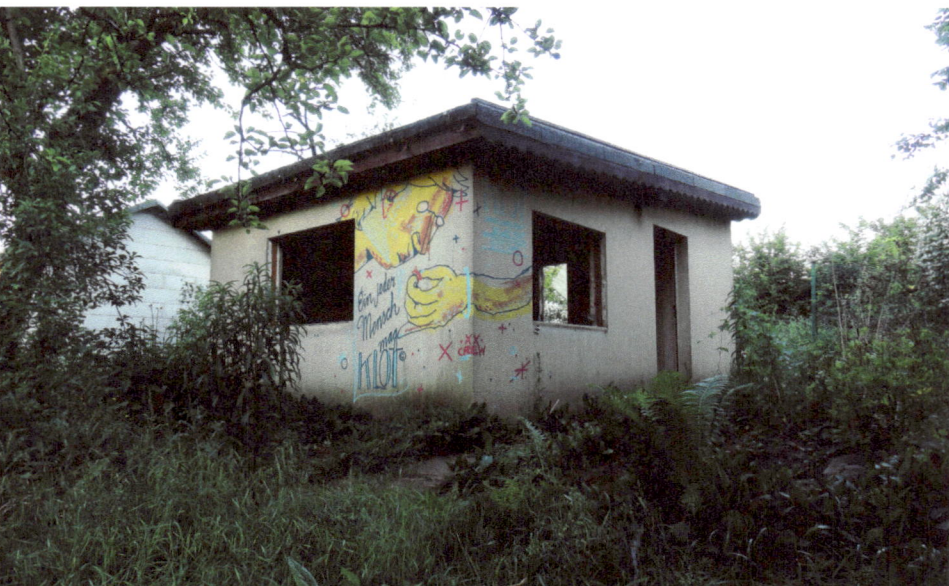
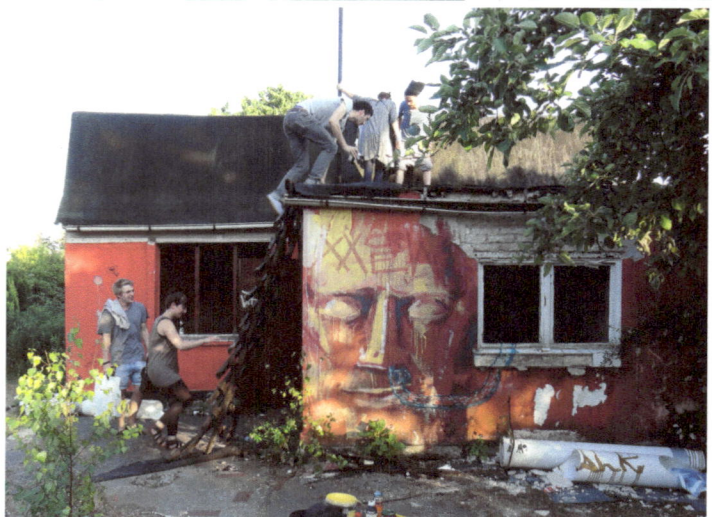
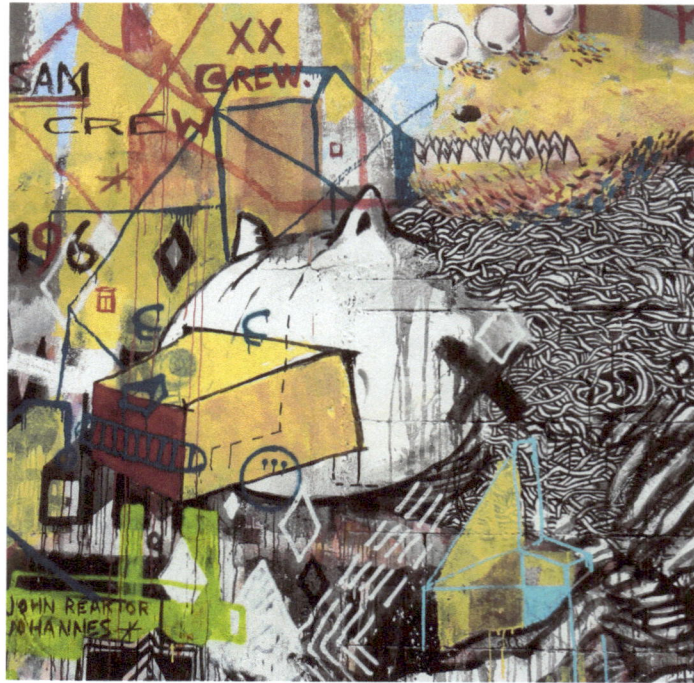

with Gregor Gonsior, Patu, Ragtag, Łódz 2011 / Berlin 2011
Berlin 2011 / with John Reaktor, SamCrew, Berlin 2011
with Otecki and Patu, Wrocław 2011

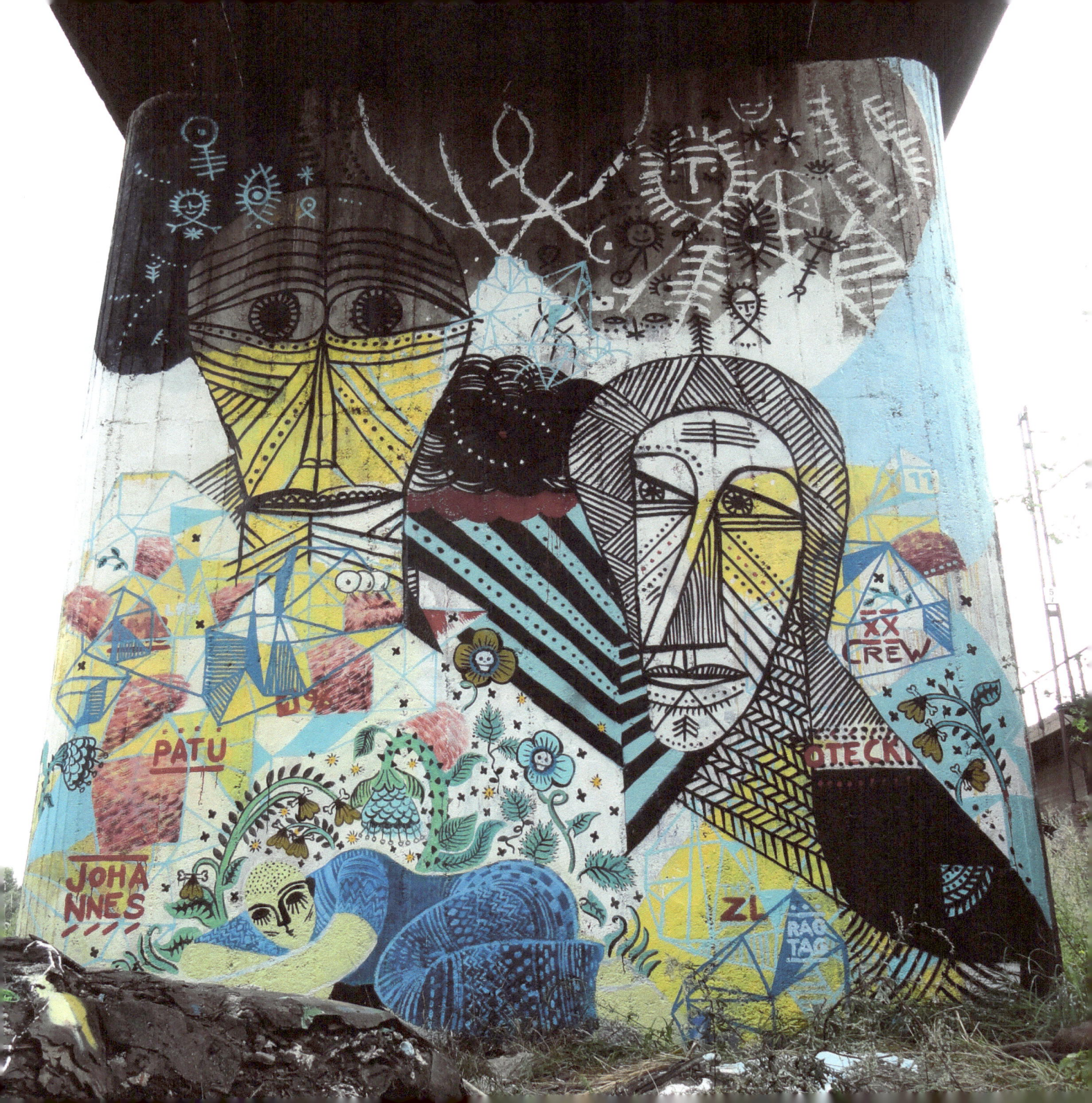

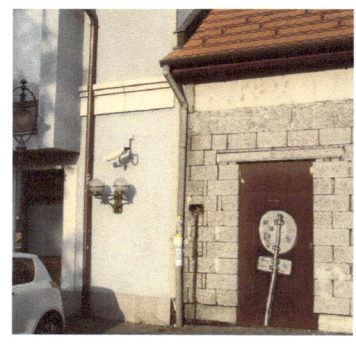 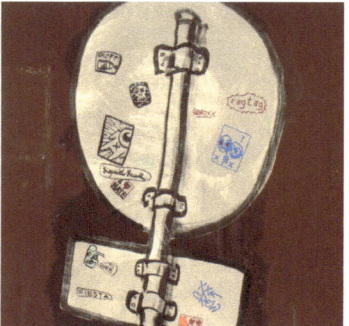 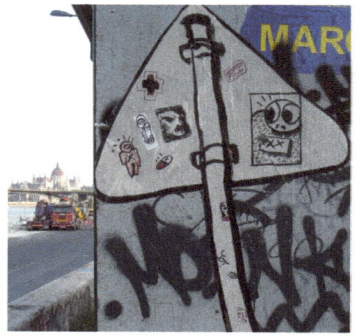 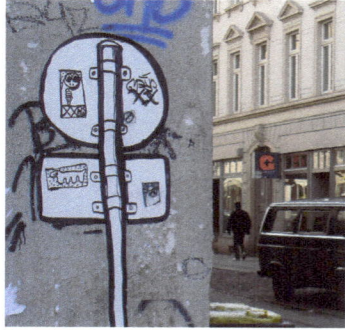

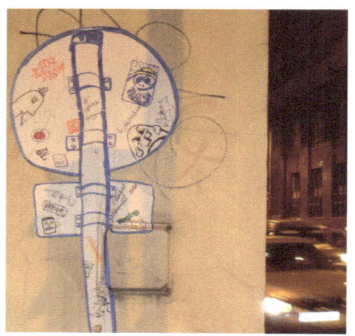 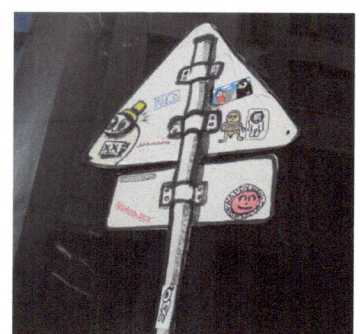 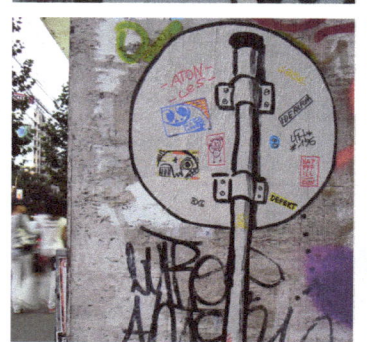 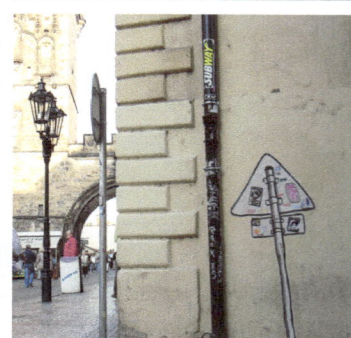

With great delight I look over and over again at the aesthetically appealing signs made by xXcrew. In addition to pure sensory pleasure they come with a sort of Kinder Surprise quality. It's because they also offer intellectual reflection and knowledge acquisition. To speak in terms of post-structuralism (and I mean it quite literally) I will now inconspicuously drop the keywords death of the author — and the consequent birth of the editor, who himself picks up samples like a DJ to weave new text patterns. Admittedly in this case, the text is yet another picture, which shouldn't bother us too much, because even school kids know: everything consists of words and there'd be no dialogue without'em. The whole thing is served with — as the French would say — "Esprit." White cut-out paper with vibrant cartoonish outlines are put up as new traffic signs in "public space" and distinctly improve the latter.

This happens casually and playfully — yet still in a sophisticated way. Not only are street art buddies and sticker pasting colleagues no longer forced to paste their work on conventional road signs so that they can revel in an extended playground — no, in self-referential coolness, the xXcrew road maintenance depot quote themselves (in keeping up with academic customs) and others well-known to cityscapes these days.
And they float my boat by doing so.

Oliver Breitenstein
Office for Ar Mediation, Münster

http://en.wikipedia.org/wiki/Death_of_the_Author

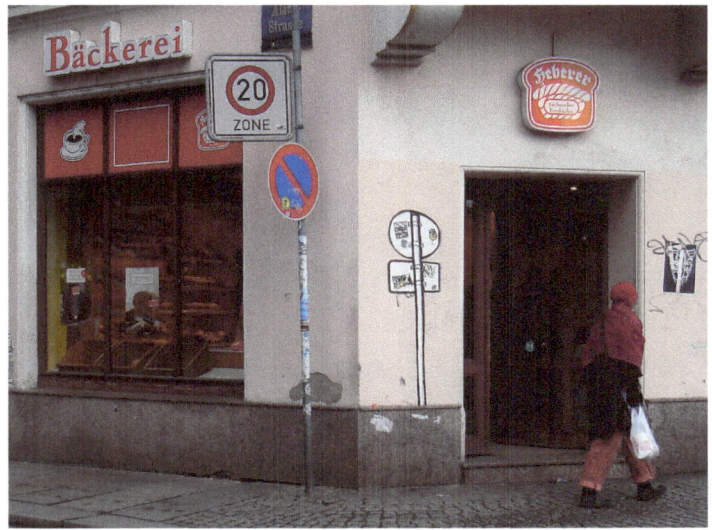
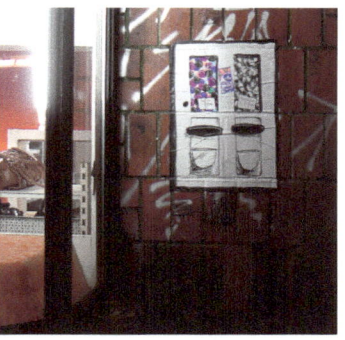
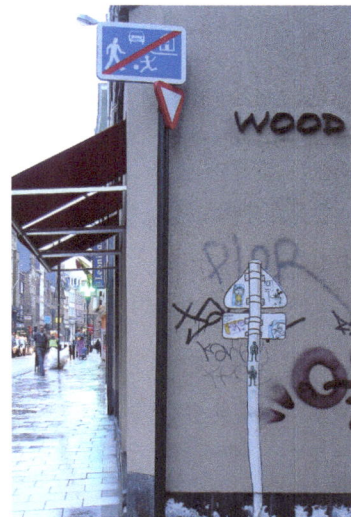
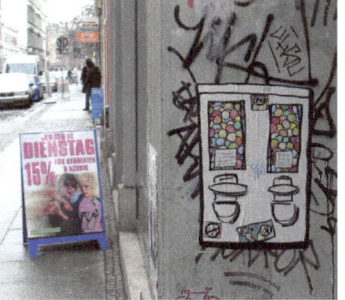
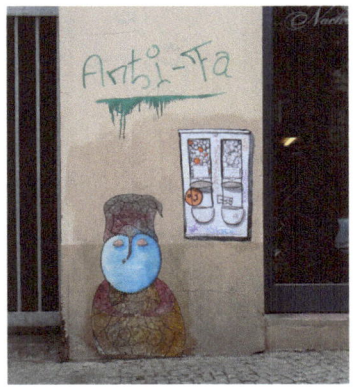
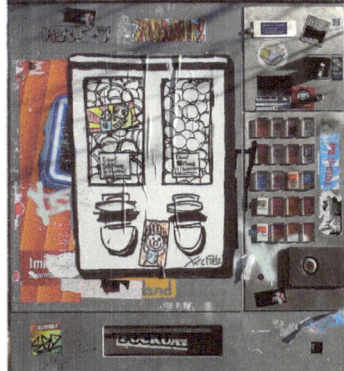
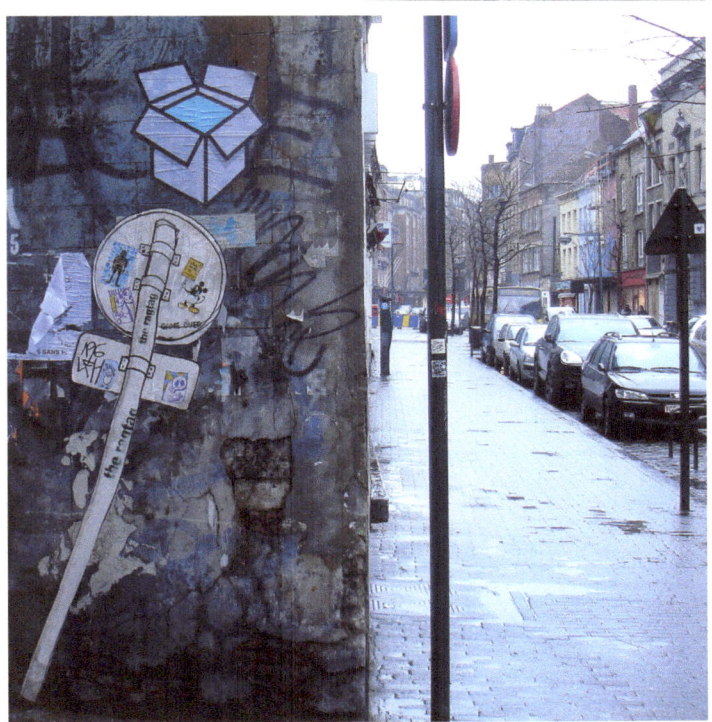

Placed at Amsterdam, Berlin, Bratislava, Brussels, Budapest,
Bucharest, Dresden, Hamburg, Münster, Offenburg, Prague.
Thank you TheRagtag!

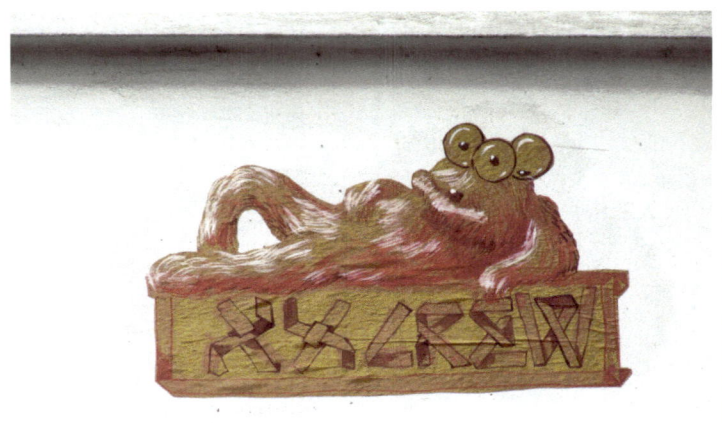

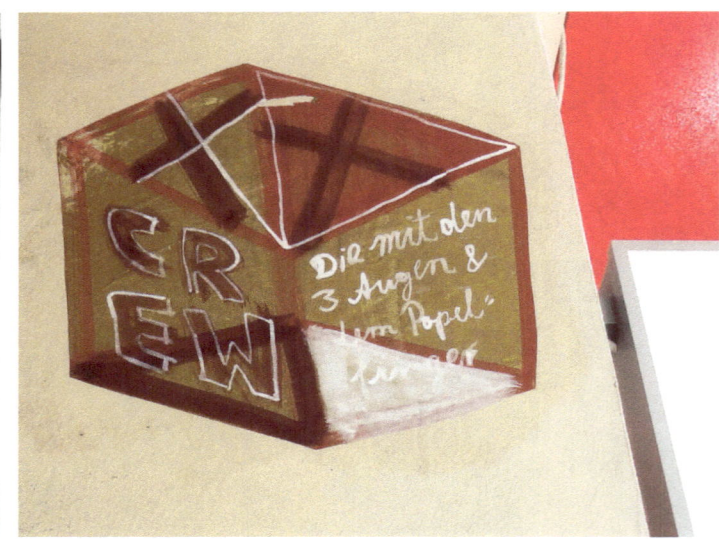

Die mit den 3 Augen & dem Popel-finger

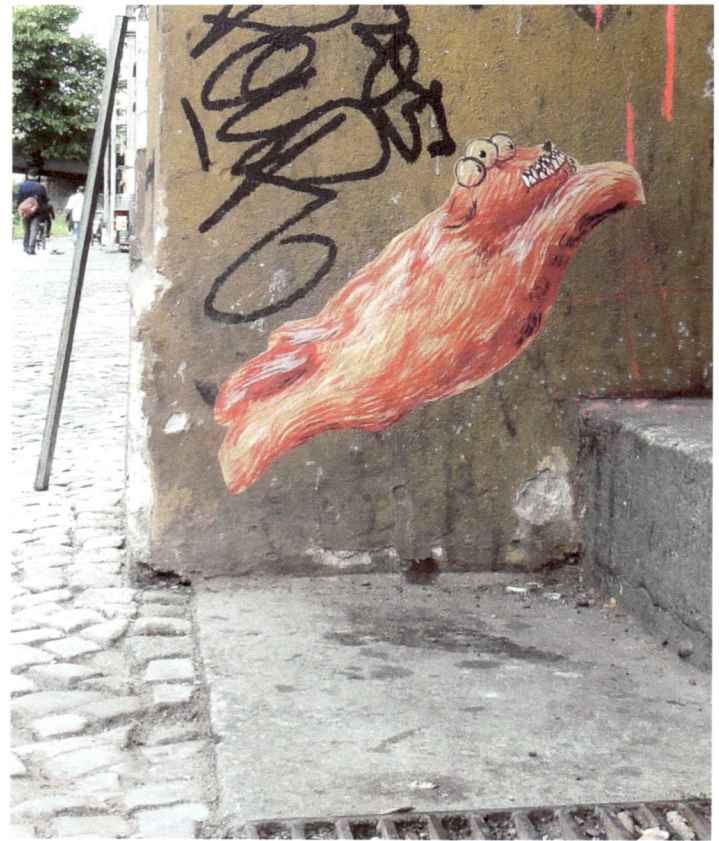

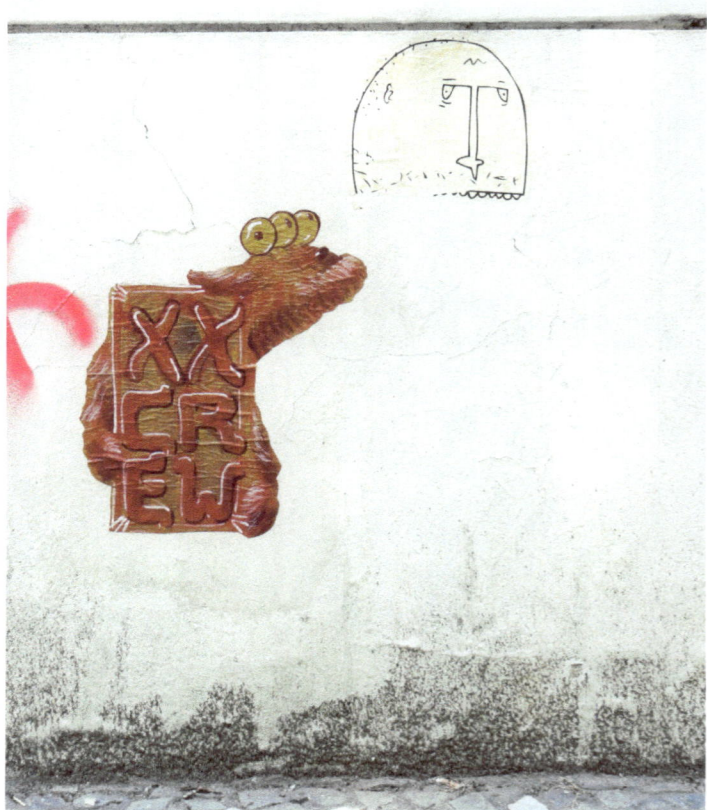

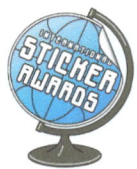
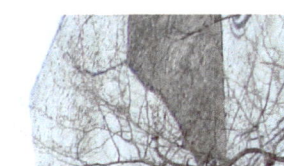

AWARDED → 3RD PLACE 2011

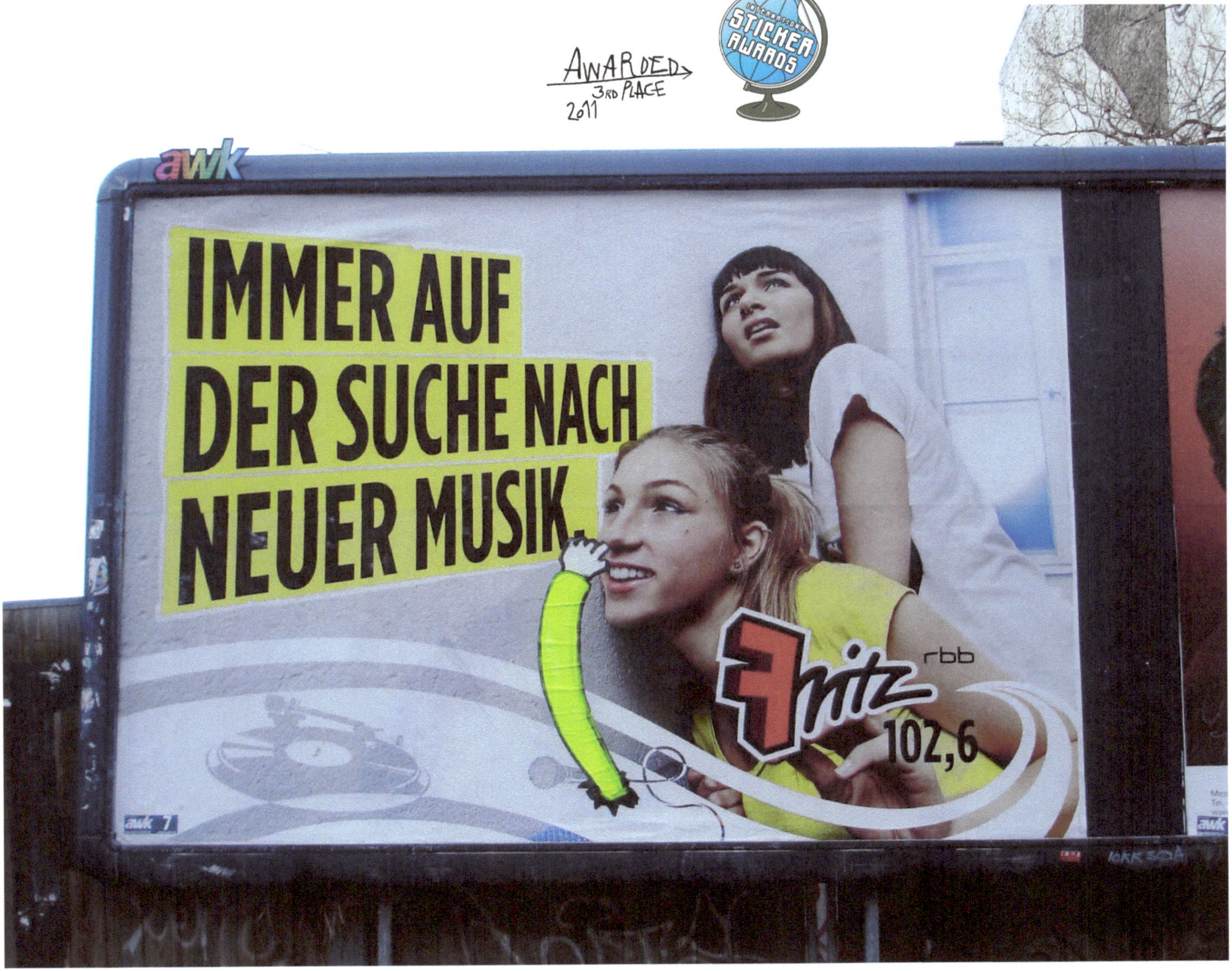

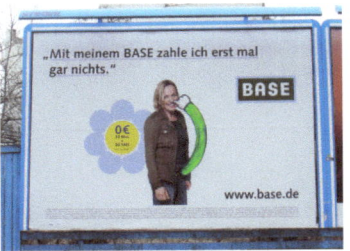
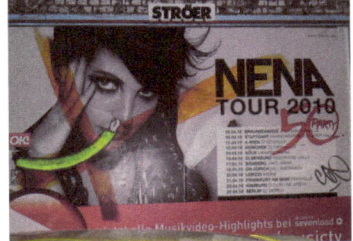
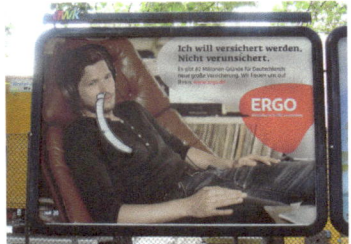
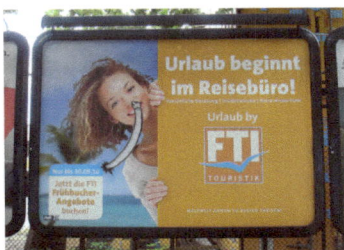

JOHANNES MUNDINGER

xXcrew

artist, curator, muralist

post@jmundinger.de
www.jmundinger.de

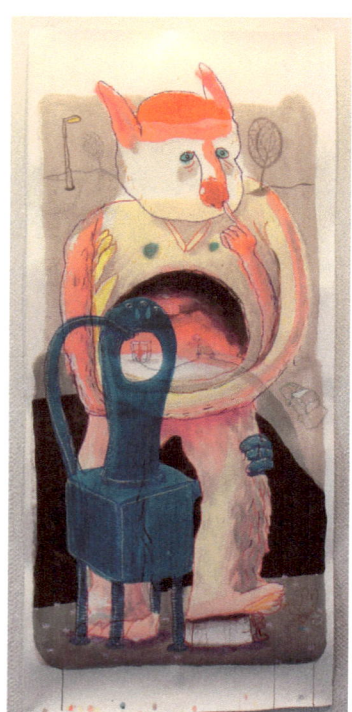

Selected exhibitions:

2012 02 His Most Exquisite Elaborations, idrawalot, Berlin

2011 12 Seven Sided Cube, Cube54, Berlin
2011 11 Sticker in der Kunst, Museum Weserburg, Bremen
2011 09 Urban Art. The New Contemporary Art, Kunstverein, Freiburg
2011 06 Puff The Magic Dragon, ExPuff, Berlin
2011 04/05 Encore et Toujours, Centre Culturel, Dinant, Belgium
2011 02 Diplomausstellung, Faculty of Design, FH Münster

2010 10 Zacusca Urban Arts, Triptychon, Münster
2010 10 Cardboarding, Cuba Kultur, Münster
2010 08 Produktion Auswurf, Galerie Kreuzberg, Münster
2010 08/09 xXcrew Soloshow, Galerie Kesselhaus, Lahr
2010 06 DoppelX sonst nix, Banditen Wie Wir, Essen
2010 01 MemorieS, SpecOps, Münster

2009 12 Faboulous4plus1, Kakadu, Offenburg
2009 12 All Eyes On Art, ISW, Freiburg
2009 12 Dreizehn Wege zum Beinbruch, Treppenhaus of Modern Art, Münster
2009 11 Asuel, Offspace, Münster
since 2009 10 Polly Pocket Museum of Modern Art, Berliner Kunstverein, Münster/Berlin
2009 09 Galerie Kreuzberg, Münster
2009 08 Verfolgungsjagd 2.0, Cuba, Münster
2009 08 Mark On Society, Raum für Kunst, Paderborn
2009 01 Links Liens, Brussels

2008 12 Mystery Christmas Exchange 2008, Essen
2008 06 Ausleuchten, Haus der Niederlande im Krameramtshaus, Münster
2008 04 Licht aus – selber Leuchten, Triptychon, Münster
2008 01 Salmen, Offenburg

2007 12 White Gallery, Frankfurt
2007 10 White Gallery, Köln
2007 06 Knapp am Mittelweg vorbei, Triptychon, Münster

2006 10 Stupid Sidekicks, Triptychon, Münster

2005 10 Zwischenspeicher, Städtische Galerie, Offenburg
2005 09 Kik, Offenburg

2004 12 Insolvenza, im alten Keilbach, Offenburg

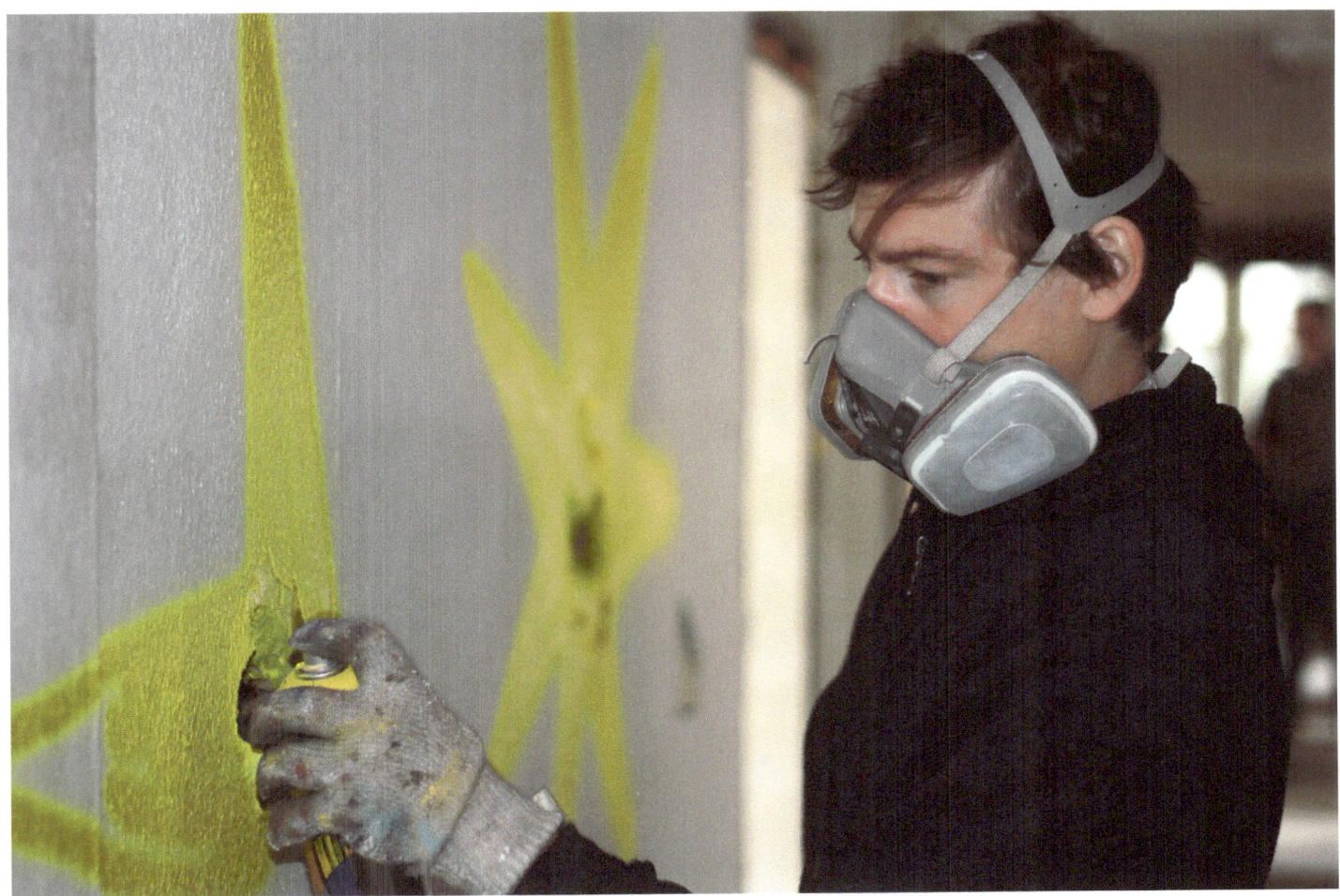

Photo by Christian Prinz

Johannes Mundinger started at Offenburg, studied at Münster and Brussels, curated at Münster and Berlin, works inside and outside.

The xXcrew is a collective of eight illustrators, photographers, graphic, fine and graffiti-artists. Founded in 2003, the connection is the result of a deep friendship and the will to change the look of public space.

Wos1, Offenburg * Volker#1, Paderborn * TheErolGuys, Freiburg * Slurg, Toronto *
Rich, Lahr * Pio Rahner, Essen * Johannes Mundinger, Berlin * Happypill, Münster

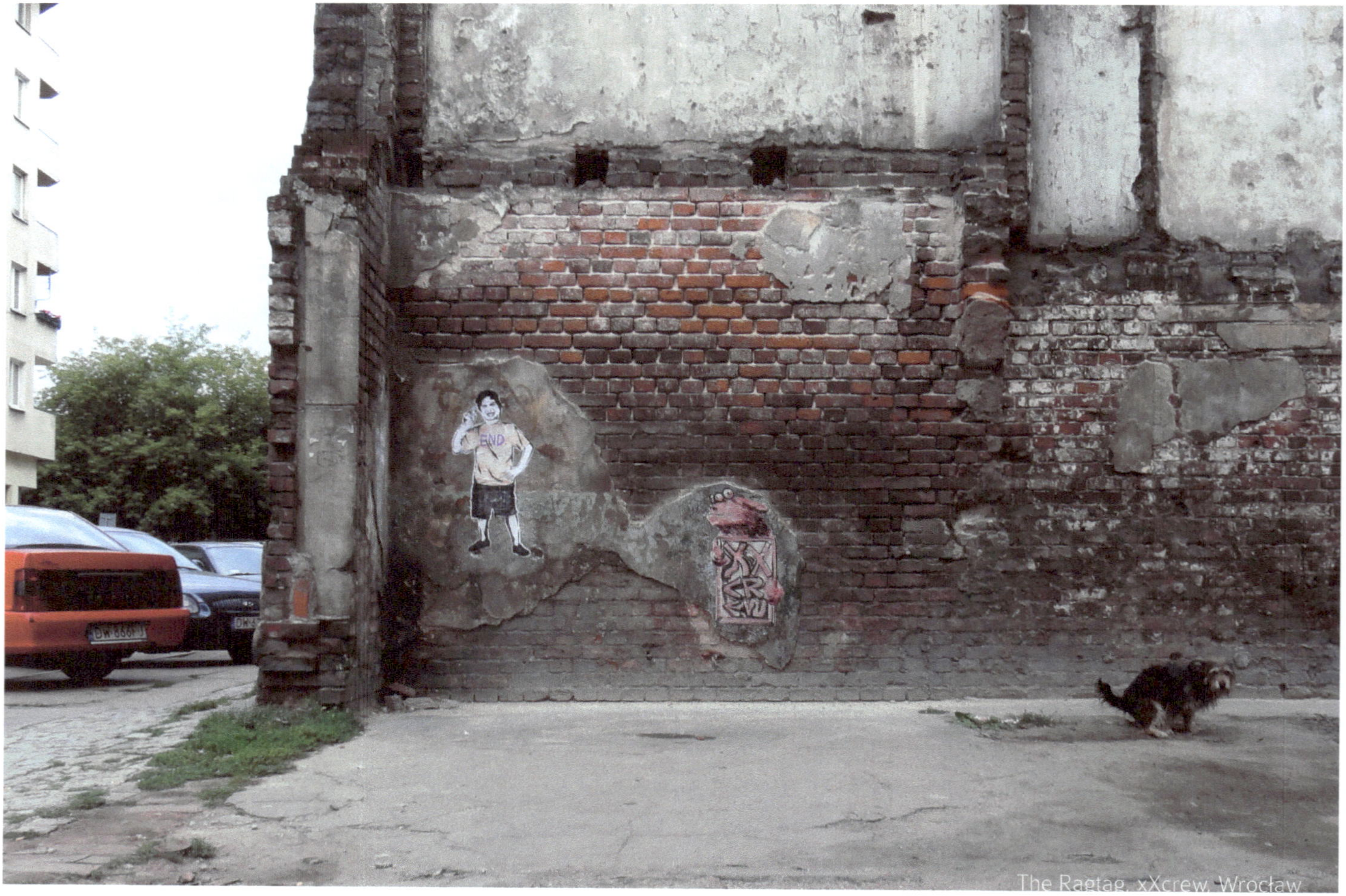

The Ragtag. xXcrew. Wrocław

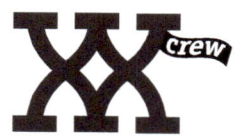

idrawalot

www.ingramcontent.com/pod-product-compliance
Lightning Source LLC
Chambersburg PA
CBHW051106180526

45172CB00002B/797